BOA
EDITIONS LTD

T0163954

This Number Does Not Exist

माँ की तस्वीर

घर में माँ की कोई तस्वीर नहीं
जब भी तस्वीर खिंचवाने का मौक़ा आता है
माँ घर में खोई हुई किसी चीज़ को ढूँढ रही होती है
या लकड़ी घास और पानी लेने गयी होती है
जंगल में उसे एक बार बाघ भी मिला
लेकिन वह डरी नहीं
उसने बाघ को भगाया घास काटी घर आकर
आग जलायी और सबके लिए खाना पकाया

मैं कभी घास या लकड़ी लाने जंगल नहीं गया
कभी आग नहीं जलायी
मैं अक्सर एक ज़माने से चली आ रही
पुरानी नक्काशीदार कुर्सी पर बैठता हूँ
जिस पर बैठकर तस्वीरें खिंचवाई जाती हैं
माँ के चेहरे पर मुझे दिखाई देती है
एक जंगल की तस्वीर लकड़ी घास और
पानी की तस्वीर
खोई हुई एक चीज़ की तस्वीर।

मंगलेश डबराल

This Number Does Not Exist

Poems by

Mangalesh Dabral

Translated from the Hindi by
Nirupama Dutt
Sarabjeet Garcha
Robert Hueckstedt
Akhil Katyal
Vishnu Khare
Arvind Krishna Mehrotra
Christi Merrill
Girdhar Rathi
Sudeep Sen
Rupert Snell
Asad Zaidi

BOA Editions, Ltd. ◆ Rochester, NY ◆ 2016

First Edition
16 17 18 19 7 6 5 4 3 2 1

Publications by BOA Editions, Ltd.—a not-for-profit corporation under section 501 (c)
(3) of the United States Internal Revenue Code—are made possible with funds from a
variety of sources, including public funds from the Literature Program of the National
Endowment for the Arts; the New York State Council on the Arts, a state agency; and the
County of Monroe, NY. Private funding sources include the Lannan Foundation for sup-
port of the Lannan Translations Selection Series; the Max and Marian Farash Charita-
ble Foundation; the Mary S. Mulligan Charitable Trust; the Rochester Area Community
Foundation; the Steeple-Jack Fund; the Ames-Amzalak Memorial Trust in memory of
Henry Ames, Semon Amzalak, and Dan Amzalak; and contributions from many indi-
viduals nationwide.

Cover Design: Sandy Knight
Cover Art: *Cover 3* by Patricia Buckley
Interior Design and Composition: Richard Foerster
BOA Logo: Mirko

Library of Congress Cataloging-in-Publication Data

Names: Dabral, Mangalesh, 1948– author.
Title: This number does not exist : poems / by Mangalesh Dabral.
Description: First edition. | Rochester, NY : BOA Editions Ltd., 2016. |
  Series: Lannan Translations Selection Series
Identifiers: LCCN 2016002301 (print) | LCCN 2016008556 (ebook) | ISBN
  9781942683124 | ISBN 9781942683131 (E-book)
Subjects: | BISAC: POETRY / Asian. | FOREIGN LANGUAGE STUDY / Hindi. |
  SOCIAL SCIENCE / Social Classes. | SOCIAL SCIENCE / Developing Countries.
Classification: LCC PK2098.19.A25 A2 2016 (print) | LCC PK2098.19.A25
  (ebook)
  | DDC 891.4/317—dc23
LC record available at http://lccn.loc.gov/2016002301

Lannan
BOA Editions, Ltd.
250 North Goodman Street, Suite 306
Rochester, NY 14607
www.boaeditions.org
A. Poulin, Jr., Founder (1938–1996)

for dearest daughter Alma

Contents

Author's Note	11
एक जीवन के लिए	14
Good for a Lifetime	15
घर शांत है	16
The Quiet House	17
पत्तों की मृत्यु	18
The Death of Leaves	19
शब्द	20
Words	21
प्रेम करती स्त्री	22
Woman in Love	23
बाहर	24
Outside	25
दादा की तस्वीर	26
Grandfather's Photograph	27
बच्चों के लिए चिट्ठी	28
Letter to Children	29
सपने की कविता	30
Poem of Dreams	31
कागज़ की कविता	32
Poem of Paper	33
आवाज़ें	34
The Sounds	35
आते-जाते	36
In Passing	37
शहर	40
City	41
दूसरा हाथ	42
The Other Hand	43
दिनचर्या	44
Daily Grind	45

हम	48
We	49
दिल्ली-2	50
Delhi: 2	51
पहाड़ पर लालटेन	52
Lantern on Mountain	53
थकान	56
Exhaustion	57
बच्चा	58
A Child	59
आख़िरी वारदात	60
Final Incident	61
वापसी	64
Return	65
सात दिन का सफ़र	66
The Seven-Day Journey	67
बचपन की कविता	68
A Poem on Childhood	69
यहाँ थी वह नदी	70
This Is Where the River Was	71
तुम्हारे भीतर	72
Inside You	73
अनुपस्थिति	74
Absence	75
प्रेम	76
Love	77
कमरा	78
The Room	79
त्वचा	80
Skin	81
ऐसा समय	82
These Times	83
दिल्ली - एक	84
Delhi: 1	85

बची हुई जगहें	86
The Places That Are Left	87
मैं चाहता हूं	88
I Wish	89
चुंबन	90
Kiss	91
न्यू आर्लींस में जैज़	92
New Orleans Jazz	93
संगतकार	96
The Accompanist	97
पिता की तस्वीर	98
A Picture of Father	99
मां की तस्वीर	100
A Picture of Mother	101
अपनी तस्वीर	102
A Picture of Myself	103
गुणानंद पथिक	104
Gunanand Pathik	105
दो कवियों की कथा	108
Tale of Two Poets	109
घर का रास्ता	110
The Way Home	111
सोने से पहले	112
Before Going to Sleep	113
छुओ	114
Touch	115
यह नंबर मौजूद नहीं	116
This Number Does Not Exist	117
गुमशुदा	118
The Missing	119
छूट गया है	120
Song of the Dislocated	121
इन सर्दियों में	122
This Winter	123

पुरानी तस्वीरें 124
Old Photographs 125

प्रतिकार 126
My Way 127

टॉर्च 128
Torchlight 129

सपना 130
A Dream 131

अभिनय 132
An Act 133

चेहरा 134
My Face 135

सभ्यता 136
Civilization 137

तस्वीर 138
A Picture 139

मांगना 140
Asking for Favors 141

शहर फिर से 142
The City, Again 143

नये युग में शत्रु 146
Enemy in the New Era 147

नया बैंक 150
The New Bank 151

गुजरात के मृतक का बयान 152
One of Gujarat's Dead Speaks 153

यथार्थ इन दिनों 156
Reality These Days 157

Acknowledgments 161
About the Author 162
About the Translators 165

Author's Note

Making a selection from one's own poems is a perplexing task. One of the reasons for this is that if a poem is good or pertinent then it parts company with its creator and starts living a life of its own no matter how long or short it may be. As for bad poems, they are as good as ash. In my language there are poems that are so independent in disposition that we can treasure them even without bringing their authors to mind. For instance, "Saroj-smriti" ("Saroj: In Memoriam") and "Wah Todati Patthar" ("A Woman Breaking Stones") are the great poet Nirala's compositions, but they lead an independent cultural and readerly life after breaking free from the poet's titular rights. Not all poems are fortunate enough to attain such significance, but what holds true for all poems is that, with the passage of time, the poet cannot have such authority on them as he or she had at the time of writing them, and the attempt to make them the poet's private property again seems like a trespass.

About forty-five years ago, when I came to Delhi with a few poems, mine was a migration from a serene, hemmed-in place endowed by nature to a sprawling and predatory world abuzz with activity. I, along with my friends, had found a city within this city and we lived in the hinterland of bright lights in a corner of semi-darkness. Despite the hardships I had to face to make ends meet, I was readily accepted in the world of poetry, maybe because the poems of a novice like me spoke of experiences that the contemporary Hindi world wasn't much familiar with. The Delhi of that time throbbed with intellectual unease: the disillusionment with the big dream of the Nehruvian era, Ram Manohar Lohia's anti-establishment views, the Beat generation of American poetry, Allen Ginsberg's journey to India, the Beatles, Hindi poet Muktibodh's death and in its wake the centrality his poetry acquired, the slogan *Mera naam tera naam, Vietnam* (my name your name is Vietnam) vehemently opposing the American attack on Vietnam, the revolutionary spirit of Naxalbari, Bengal's Hungry generation, the Digambar Rachayithalu Sangham (Naked Writers' Association) in Telugu, the Dalit Panther movement in Marathi poetry; all these images merged to form the backdrop of a seemingly imminent change. The cerebral waves of that time were very steep and had swept in the people of my generation from near and far. Most good poetry witnessed and recorded the temperature of those heated times and sided mostly with the forces opposed to power structures.

My poetry was born in the mountains, lived among the stones, and sang of water, clouds, trees, and birds; but soon it migrated to the cities where the world was not so simple and innocent despite all its attractions, its wide and ever-lit roads, squares and lampposts, which looked like the signifiers of a new civilization. It was filled with the strains between the loss of native spaces and the difficulties of coming to terms with the place of refuge. In fact, dislocation due to various natural and man-made factors (which marks one of the basic attributes of our post-Independence generation) and encounters with anomalous realities remain recurrent themes in my poetic creations as well as those of my generation. As I turn back and look at my first collection, *Pahar par Laltein* (*Lantern on the Mountain*), I see in it a strange coexistence of the country and the city, of memories of leaving the clear skies of my native hills and entering the dust of a terrain hitherto unknown. But the memory served as imagination for my poetic efforts, and the concrete became the scaffolding for the abstract.

My generation has also been fortunate because many poets who had played a vital role in shaping modern Hindi poetry and its conscience were quite active at that time. There were poets like Shamsher Bahadur Singh, Nagarjun, Trilochan, Ajneya, Kedarnath Agarwal and, after them, Raghuvir Sahay, Kunwar Narain, Sarveshwar Dayal Saxena, and Dhoomil, to name a few. Around the same period, Muktibodh's long poem "Andhere mein" ("In Darkness") was rediscovered as a seminal composition depicting the post-Independence sociocultural and political nightmare. This poem became a metaphorical text and a reference point of our time. Alongside Muktibodh, Shamsher introduced us to the mysteries and interior landscapes of poetry, whereas from Nagarjun and Raghuvir Sahay we learned how to observe and dissect the human ironies of our democracy in rural and urban spaces.

The Italian Marxist thinker Antonio Gramsci considered "pessimism of the intellect and optimism of the will" as characteristic of the essential or "organic" intellectual, as he called it. My poetry, too, intended to hold both the ends of this very hopelessness and hope, and despite its despairing undertones, it tried to drench itself in optimism. Sometimes it even drew strength from the pessimistic experiences it came across in a society fraught with so many inequalities, injustices, and subhuman conditions. It wanted to respond to contemporary times as well as transcend them and create a better, more humane world—an anti-world which may be more livable. Such a world that's free of oppression, global barbarism, and hegemonies may not be possible, but poetry always strives to achieve some semblance of these qualities.

When I set about choosing poems from my five collections published so far, I realized how far away I had moved from them, and then remembered a famous quote from Anton Chekhov's play *The Three Sisters*: "If one life, which has been already lived, were only a rough sketch so to speak, and the second were the final copy! Then, I think, every one of us would try before anything else not to repeat himself." I thought, how nice it would be if I could take my old poems as rough copies, revise them, and give them a second life. But is it possible to create them afresh? We all know that nothing comes back and nothing happens twice.

At times, I wonder about the role of poetry in the life of a society. Does poetry save anything? What use is it to humankind? The Russian poet Vladimir Mayakovsky, while referring to the need for poetry, said that if flowers blossom and stars shine, then it simply means that somebody needs them. The impact of poetry, its humanizing effect, may not be directly visible or concrete, but once I was led to think otherwise by a tribal domestic worker in Gujarat. The dark-complexioned girl, Tina Naika, had decided to take her life because of personal dejection, but gave up the thought after reading one of my poems that was prescribed in her Hindi curriculum. Small incidents like this one reaffirmed my faith in the role poetry silently plays in people's lives in times of sorrow, hopelessness, and injustice. And just imagine what kind of society it'd have been if poetry hadn't existed!

Mangalesh Dabral
Christmas 2015
New Delhi

एक जीवन के लिए

शायद वहां थोड़ी-सी नमी थी
या हल्का-सा कोई रंग
शायद सिहरन या उम्मीद

शायद वहां एक आंसू था
या एक चुंबन
याद रखने के लिए
शायद वहां बर्फ़ थी
या छोटा-सा एक हाथ
या सिर्फ़ छूने की कोशिश

शायद अंधेरा था
या एक ख़ाली मैदान
या खड़े होने भर की जगह
शायद वहां एक आदमी था
अपने ही तरीक़े से लड़ता हुआ.

Good for a Lifetime

Perhaps there was a bit of moisture there
or a pastel shade
Perhaps a shiver, perhaps hope

Perhaps there was just one teardrop there
or, as a keepsake,
a kiss
Perhaps there was snow there
or a small hand
or the attempt to touch

Perhaps there was darkness there
or an open field
or standing room

Perhaps there was a man there
struggling in his own way.

translated by Arvind Krishna Mehrotra

घर शांत है

धूप दीवारों को धीरे-धीरे गर्म कर रही है
आसपास एक धीमी आंच है
बिस्तर पर एक गेंद पड़ी है
किताबें चुपचाप हैं
हालांकि उनमें कई तरह की विपदाएं बंद हैं

मैं अधजगा हूं और अधसोया हूं
अधसोया हूं और अधजगा हूं
बाहर से आती आवाज़ों में
किसी के रोने की आवाज़ नहीं है
किसी के धमकाने या डरने की आवाज़ नहीं है
न कोई प्रार्थना कर रहा है
न कोई भीख मांग रहा है

और मेरे भीतर ज़रा भी मैल नहीं है
बल्कि एक ख़ाली जगह है
जहां कोई रह सकता है
और मैं लाचार नहीं हूं इस समय
बल्कि भरा हुआ हूं एक ज़रूरी वेदना से
और मुझे याद आ रहा है बचपन का घर
जिसके आंगन में औंधा पड़ा मैं
पीठ पर धूप सेंकता था

मैं दुनिया से कुछ नहीं मांग रहा हूं
मैं जी सकता हूं गिलहरी गेंद
या घास जैसा कोई जीवन
मुझे चिंता नहीं
कब कोई झटका हिलाकर ढहा देगा
इस शांत घर को.

The Quiet House

The sun by slow degrees heats up the walls,
Somewhere close by a slow fire burns,
There's a ball lying on the bed,
Books, despite the misfortunes
They contain, are silent.
I'm half awake, half asleep,
Half asleep, half awake,
Listening to outside sounds,
No one crying,
Or giving a threat, or pleading,
No one praying,
No one asking for alms.
And there's no bitterness in me,
Just an empty space
For someone to come and fill,
Nor do I feel helpless
But an ache spreads through my body
As I recall the house of my childhood
In whose courtyard, lying on my stomach,
I would take the sun.
I ask nothing of the world,
And can live as squirrels do,
As grass does, or a ball,
Not at all worried
That at any moment someone can shake this house
And bring it down.

translated by Arvind Krishna Mehrotra

पत्तों की मृत्यु

कितने सारे पत्ते उड़कर आते हैं
चेहरे पर मेरे बचपन के पेड़ों से
एक झील अपनी लहरें
मुझ तक भेजती है
लहर की तरह कांपती है रात
और उस पर मैं चलता हूं
चेहरे पर पत्तों की मृत्यु लिये हुए

चिड़ियां अपने हिस्से की आवाज़ें
कर चुकी हैं लोग जा चुके हैं
रोशनियां राख हो चुकी हैं
सड़क के दोनों ओर
घरों के दरवाज़े बंद हैं
मैं आवाज़ देता हूं
और वह लौट आती है मेरे पास.

The Death of Leaves

The leaves that settle on my face
Fall from my childhood's trees.
A lake sends me its waves, and,
Like a wave, the night quivers. I walk
On it, the death of leaves on my face.

The birds have made their sounds.
The place is empty. The lights
Are ash. The houses on either side
Of the road have locked front doors.
I call out, and my voice rebounds.

translated by Arvind Krishna Mehrotra

शब्द

कुछ शब्द चीख़ते हैं
कुछ कपड़े उतारकर
घुस जाते हैं इतिहास में
कुछ हो जाते हैं ख़ामोश.

Words

Some words scream
Some take off their clothes
And barge into history
Some fall silent.

translated by Arvind Krishna Mehrotra

प्रेम करती स्त्री

प्रेम करती स्त्री देखती है
एक सपना रोज़
जागने पर सोचती है क्या था वह
निकालने बैठती है अर्थ

दिखती हैं उसे आमफ़हम चीज़ें
कोई रेतीली जगह
लगातार बहता नल
उसकी घर बिखरा हुआ
देखती है कुछ है जो दिखलाई नहीं पड़ता
कई बार देखने के बाद

प्रेम करती स्त्री
यक़ीन नहीं करती किसी का
कंघा गिरा देती है
दर्पण में नहीं देखती ख़ुद को
सोचती है मैं ऐसे ही हूं ठीक

उसकी सहेलियां एक-एक कर
उसे छोड़कर चली जाती हैं
धूप उसके पास आये बिना निकल जाती है
हवा उसके बाल बिखराये बिना बहती है
उसके खाये बिना हो जाता है खाना ख़त्म

प्रेम करती स्त्री
ठगी जाती है रोज़
उसे पता नहीं चलता बाहर क्या हो रहा है
कौन ठग रहा है कौन है खलनायक
पता नहीं चलता कहां से शुरू हुई कहानी

दुनिया को समझती है वह
गोद में बैठा हुआ बच्चा
निकल जाती है अकेली सड़क पर
देखती है कितना बड़ा फैला शहर
सोचती है मैं रह लूंगी यहां कहीं.

Woman in Love

The woman in love
Has this dream every night.
What's it about? One morning,
She decides to find out.
Around her she sees the most ordinary things:
Sandy ground,
A tap left running,
Her disarrayed room,
And something she can see
She cannot see, though she looks again.
The woman in love
Trusts no one.
She lets go of her comb
And turns her back to the mirror.
She says, I'm okay as I am.
One by one her friends desert her.
The sun goes down, keeping its distance.
The wind blows, but not through her hair.
The table is cleared
Without her having eaten.
The woman in love
Is deceived every day.
She doesn't know what's happening outside,
Who the cheat is, who takes her for a ride.
She doesn't know how it all began.
The world's a child in my arms,
Says the woman in love.
She comes out on the road alone
And looks at the big city around her.
Somewhere or other, she says, I'll find a place to live.

translated by Arvind Krishna Mehrotra

बाहर

मैंने दरवाज़े बंद किये
और कविता लिखने बैठा
बाहर हवा चल रही थी
हल्की रोशनी थी
बारिश में एक साइकिल खड़ी थी
एक बच्चा घर लौट रहा था

मैंने कविता लिखी
जिसमें हवा नहीं थी बच्चा नहीं था
दरवाज़े नहीं थे.

Outside

I closed the door
and sat down to write a poem
outside a breeze was blowing
there was a little light
a bicycle stood in the rain
a child was coming home
I wrote a poem
which had no breeze no light
no bicycle no child
and
no door.

translated by Arvind Krishna Mehrotra

दादा की तस्वीर

दादा को तस्वीरें खिंचवाने का शौक़ नहीं था
या उन्हें समय नहीं मिला
उनकी सिर्फ़ एक तस्वीर गंदी पुरानी दीवार पर टंगी है
वे शांत और गंभीर बैठे हैं
पानी से भरे हुए बादल की तरह

दादा के बारे में इतना ही मालूम है
कि वे मांगनेवालों को भीख देते थे
नींद में बेचैनी से करवट बदलते थे
और सुबह उठकर
बिस्तर की सलवटें ठीक करते थे
मैं तब बहुत छोटा था
मैंने कभी उनकी गुस्सा नहीं देखा
उनकी मामूलीपन नहीं देखा
तस्वीरें किसी मनुष्य की लाचारी नहीं बतलातीं
मां कहती है जब हम
रात के विचित्र पशुओं से घिरे सो रहे होते हैं
दादा इस तस्वीर में जागते रहते हैं

मैं अपने दादा जितना लंबा नहीं हुआ
शांत और गंभीर नही हुआ
पर मुझमें कुछ है उनसे मिलता-जुलता
वैसा ही क्रोध वैसा ही मामूलीपन
मैं भी सिर झुकाकर चलता हूं
जीता हूं अपने को एक तस्वीर के ख़ाली फ्रेम में
बैठे देखता हुआ.

Grandfather's Photograph

Grandfather wasn't fond of being photographed
or didn't find time perhaps
There's just one picture of him
hanging on an old discolored wall
He sits serious and composed
like a cloud heavy with water
All we know of Grandfather is
that he gave alms to beggars
tossed restlessly in sleep
and made his bed neatly every morning
I was just a kid then
and never saw his anger or
his ordinariness
Pictures never show someone's helpless side
Mother used to tell us that
when we fell asleep surrounded
by strange creatures of the night
Grandfather would stay awake inside the picture
I didn't grow as tall as Grandfather
not as composed or as serious
Still something in me resembles him
An anger like his
an ordinariness
I too walk with my head bent down
and every day see myself
sitting in an empty
picture frame.

translated by Arvind Krishna Mehrotra

बच्चों के लिए चिट्ठी

प्यारे बच्चो हम तुम्हारे काम नहीं आ सके. तुम चाहते थे हमारा क़ीमती समय तुम्हारे खेलों में व्यतीत हो. तुम चाहते थे हम तुम्हें अपने खेलों मैं शरीक करें. तुम चाहते थे हम तुम्हारी तरह मासूम हो जायें.

प्यारे बच्चो हमने ही तुम्हें बताया था जीवन एक युद्धस्थल है जहां लड़ते ही रहना होता है. हम ही थे जिन्होंने हथियार पैने किये. हमने ही छेड़ा युद्ध. हम ही थे जो क्रोध और घृणा से बौखलाते थे. प्यारे बच्चो हमने तुमसे झूठ कहा था.

यह एक लंबी रात है. एक सुरंग की तरह. यहां से हम देख सकते हैं बाहर का एक अस्पष्ट दृश्य. हम देखते हैं मारकाट और विलाप. बच्चो हमने ही तुम्हें वहां भेजा था. हमें माफ़ कर दो. हमने झूठ कहा था कि जीवन एक युद्धस्थल है.

प्यारे बच्चो जीवन एक उत्सव है जिसमें तुम हंसी की तरह फैले हो. जीवन एक हरा पेड़ है जिस पर तुम चिड़ियों की तरह फड़फड़ाते हो. जैसा कि कुछ कवियों ने कहा है जीवन एक उछलती गेंद है और तुम उसके चारों ओर एकत्र चंचल पैरों की तरह हो.

प्यारे बच्चो अगर ऐसा नहीं है तो होना चाहिए.

Letter to Children

Dear children, we could do nothing for you. You wanted us to join in your games, and you wanted to play ours, you wanted us to become innocent like yourselves.

Dear children, we told you living was a war without end. We sharpened the knives and were the first to use them. Hatred and anger made us blind. Dear children we lied to you.

This has been a long night, long as a tunnel, and though the view outside is clouded, we hear the weeping. Children forgive us for sending you there. We lied when we said life was a battleground.

Dear children, life's a festival through which you spread like laughter, it's a green tree, and you the birds fluttering inside it; it's a tossed ball, as the poets say, and you the restless feet that surround it.

Dear children, if it's not so then it ought to be.

translated by Arvind Krishna Mehrotra

सपने की कविता

सपने उन अनिवार्य नतीजों में से हैं जिन पर हमारा कोई नियंत्रण नहीं होता. वे हमारे अर्धजीवन को पूर्णता देने के लिए आते हैं. सपने में ही हमें दिखता है कि हम पहले क्या थे या कि आगे चलकर क्या होंगे. जीवन के एक गोलार्ध में जब हम हांफते हुए दौड़ लगा रहे होते हैं तो दूसरे गोलार्ध में सपने हमें किसी जगह चुपचाप सुलाये रहते हैं.

सपने में हमें पृथ्वी गोल दिखाई देती है जैसा कि हमने बचपन को किताबों में पढ़ा था. सूरज तेज़ गर्म महसूस होता है और तारे अपने ठंढे प्रकाश में सिहरते रहते हैं. हम देखते हैं चारों ओर ख़ुशी के पेड़. सामने से एक साइकिल गुज़रती है या कहीं से रेडियो की आवाज़ सुनाई देती है. सपने में हमें दिखती हैं अपने जीवन की जड़ें साफ़ पानी में डूबी हुईं. चांद दिखता है एक छोटे-से अंधेरे कमरे में चमकता हुआ.

सपने में हम देखते हैं कि हम अच्छे आदमी हैं. देखते हैं एक पुराना टूटा-फूटा आईना. देखते हैं हमारी नाक से बहकर आ रहा है ख़ून.

Poem of Dreams

There's no running away from dreams; they happen as a conse-
quence of waking. They tell us what we were and what we shall be-
come. They make our half lives whole. While we breathlessly rush
around one hemisphere, they keep us quietly asleep in a corner of
the other.

In dreams the earth looks round, just as our schoolbooks had said.
The sun's heat is intense and stars shiver in their cold light. Trees of
happiness grow around us. Someone on a bicycle goes by; we hear
a radio playing. We see our roots immersed in clear water. We see
the moon shining in a small dark room.

In dreams we see ourselves as righteous men. We see an old cracked
mirror. We see blood coming out our noses.

translated by Arvind Krishna Mehrotra

का़ग़ज़ की कविता

वे का़ग़ज़ जो हमारे जीवन में कभी अनिवार्य थे एक दिन रद्दी बनकर
चारों ओर जमा हो जाते हैं. जब हम सोने जाते हैं तब भी वे हमें
दिखाई देते हैं. वे हमारे स्वप्नों को रोक लेते हैं. सुबह जब हम अनिद्रा
की शिकायत करते हैं तो इसकी मुख्य वजह यही है कि हम उन
का़ग़ज़ों से घिरे सो रहे थे. चाहते हुए भी हम उन्हें बेच नहीं पाते
क्योंकि उनमें हमारे सामान्य व्यवहार दबे होते हैं जिन्हें हम अपने से
बताते हुए भी कतराते हैं. लिहाजा हम फाड़ने बैठ जाते हैं तमाम फ़ालतू
का़ग़ज़ों को.

इस तरह फाड़ दी जाती हैं पुरानी चिट्ठियां जो हमारे बुरे वक़्त में
प्रियजनों ने हमें लिखी थीं. हमारे असफल प्रेम के दस्तावेज़ चिंदी-चिंदी
हो जाते हैं. कुछ प्रमुख कवियों की कविताएं भी फट जाती हैं. नष्ट
हो चुके हैं वे शब्द जिनके बारे में हमने सोचा था कि इनसे मनुष्यता
की भूख मिटेगी. अब इन का़ग़ज़ों से किसी बच्चे की नाव भी नहीं
बन सकती और न थोड़ी दूर उड़कर वापस लौट आनेवाला जहाज़.

अब हम लगभग निश्शब्द है. हम नहीं जानते कि क्या करें. हमारे
पास कोई रास्ता नहीं बचा का़ग़ज़ों को फाड़ते रहने के सिवा.

Poem of Paper

One day we find sheets of paper that were once important scattered everywhere around us. We see them even as we go to sleep. They put an end to our dreams and cause insomnia. Our everyday lives, the things we hate to admit to ourselves, are buried in them. Which is why, much as we'd like to, we cannot even sell them to the rag-and-bone man. We have no choice except to sit down and destroy them.

This is how old letters get torn, written by sympathetic friends when we were down and out. Declarations of unrequited love, along with poems by some major poets, poems we believed would remove the world's hunger, get reduced to shreds. Now you cannot make even a paper boat or missile with them, the kind that flies a short distance and turns back.

We have become wordless, and all but lost our speech. We go on tearing the paper. It's our only hope.

translated by Arvind Krishna Mehrotra

आवाज़ें

कुछ देर बाद
शुरू होंगी आवाज़ें

पहले एक कुत्ता भूंकेगा पास से
कुछ दूर हिनहिनायेगा एक घोड़ा
बस्ती के पास सियार बोलेंगे

बीच में कहीं होगा झींगुर का बोलना
पत्तों का हिलना
बीच में कहीं होगा
रास्ते पर किसी का अकेले चलना

इन सबसे बाहर
एक बाघ के डुकरने की आवाज़
होगी मेरे गांव में.

The Sounds

Soon it will begin
to fill in with sounds

The dog's bark
up the lane the whining horse
jackals on the outskirts

Crickets chirping in between
the rustling of leaves
A solitary walk somewhere
in a lonesome street

Farther away a tiger
They would hear a roar
over my hamlet.

translated by Girdhar Rathi

आते-जाते

यहां आते-जाते मैंने
भूख के बारे में सोचा जो
दिन में तीन बार लगती थी
और चाहती थी थोड़ा-सा अन्न
कर जाती थी थोड़ा-सा पराजित
हर बार एक स्वप्न दब जाता था उसके नीचे
चेहरे पर आंखों में पूरी देह में
वह हर जगह दिखती थी गुर्राती हुई
मांगती हुई एक इच्छा का रक्त

यहां आते-जाते मैंने
ऊब के बारे में सोचा जो
मेज़ पर फैले पानी में कांपते हुए
हमारे चेहरों से टपककर फैलती जाती थी
आसपास कभी कोई आदमी दिखता था
हांफता अंधेरे में जाता हुआ
कभी कोई औरत दिखती थी
अपना डर छिपाती हुई

यहां आते-जाते मैंने
उम्मीद के बारे में सोचा
जिसे अभी कई लड़ाइयां लड़नी थीं
फ़ैसले सुनाने थे कब से किये हुए
चारों ओर एक विशाल समरांगण होना था
और बच्चों को दौड़ते हुए आना था
हवाएं चलनी थीं घंटियां बजनी थीं
हर किसी के लौट आने की सूचना देती हुईं

यहां आते-जाते मैंने
शहर के बारे में सोचा
जो पालतू सूर्यास्त और सनसनीख़ेज़ ख़बरों से
लौटकर अपने मुखौटे छिपा रहा था
किसी तरह सोने की जगह बनाते
दोस्तों से मैंने कहा
कुछ बचाया नहीं जा सकता

In Passing

Passing here now and again
I thought of hunger
that curled up
thrice a day
demanding a loaf of bread
a dream went under
leaving me a little deflated
each time it sprang up
purring and pawing
my face my eyes my entire being
demanding blood
of a mute desire

Passing here now and again
I thought of ennui
that dripped from our faces
and formed a tremulous puddle
on the table we sat around
and watched
a man would heave past us
vanishing in the dark
sometimes a woman
scurrying
hard-put to hide her fright

Passing here now and again
I thought of hope
that still had to wage wars
and pass verdicts
made ages away
a field had yet to be mapped
the children had to come
running and clapping
winds had to blow

रात में हम जो सपने देखेंगे
वे भी सुबह यहीं छूट जायेंगे
बाहर एक सड़क होगी कहीं जाती हुई
एक बस होगी हमें वहां ले जाती हुई
एक नौकरी होगी धमकाती काम कराती हुई

यहां आते-जाते
मैंने दुनिया के बारे में सोचा
जो चारों ओर से बंद और डरी हुई थी
हमारे दिमाग़ों की तरह
नंगी पड़ी चीज़ों के बाहर और भीतर
ख़ामोशी थी किताबों में
चौरस्तों पर आसमान में
कविताएं लिख-लिखकर
हम एक विशाल अंधेरे में फेंकते जाते थे
हमारे शब्दों से कितनी दूर
ज़िंदा रहते थे लोग
हमारी चीख़ से कितनी दूर मार दिये जाते थे वे
किसी मोड़ पर.

bells to toll
"all is home
safe and sound"

Passing here now and again
I thought of the city
tucking its mask away
as it returned
from the round of horrors
and a tame sunset
I said to my friends
who could barely make some roost to sleep:
Nothing can be saved
not even dreams
though a road will be there
leading somewhere
and a bus
to carry us maybe

Passing here now and again
I thought of the world
scared and sealed up it was
like our brains
a stillness reigned
in and out of the things lying bare
the books the skies the busy neighborhoods
we wrote poems
flinging them into a petulant dark
far off lived and died the people
from our words our shrieks.

translated by Girdhar Rathi

शहर

मैंने शहर को देखा और मैं मुस्कराया
वहां कोई कैसे रह सकता है
यह जानने मैं गया
और वापस न आया.

City

I looked at the city
and smiled
and walked in
who would ever want to live here
I wondered
and never went back.

translated by Girdhar Rathi

दूसरा हाथ

आख़िरकार मेरे पास एक ही हाथ है
उससे कितने काम कर सकता हूं मैं
मैंने कहा
मेरा दूसरा हाथ लगभग बेकार है
कम ही काम आता है यह किसी के
और अक्सर मुझे याद नहीं रहता
कि एक दूसरा भी हाथ है मेरे पास

इसी एक हाथ से मैं कर पाता हूं काम
मसलन आपके घर पानी भरना
आभार के शब्द लिखना
बसों की रेलिंग से लटकना
सार-संभाल करना आपके संसार की
चलते हुए मैं इस हाथ को ज़ोरों से झुलाता हूं
ताकि यह सक्रिय रहे और परवाह न करे

दूसरा हाथ तब कहीं दुबका होता है
झाड़ी के ख़रगोश-सा
या दूर बचपन की गेंदों
और लकड़ी के घोड़े बीच पड़ा हुआ
युवावस्था में किसी लड़की की हाथ भींचे हुए वह हाथ
जिसे छू नहीं पाता मेरा यह झूलता हुआ हाथ

शहरों दफ़्तरों घरों के दरवाज़े
खटखटाता जाता है यह हाथ
इसी से करने होते हैं मुझे सारे काम
दुनिया के सबसे बड़े झूठों में शुमार यह हाथ
जो थकता नहीं निराश नहीं होता कभी
जब हद हो जाती है
तब दूसरा हाथ कभी-कभी जतलाता है अपना विरोध
कांपता दर्द करता हुआ.

The Other Hand

After all I've only got one hand
and how much can you do with it?
The other hand's almost useless
not much help
and I often forget
that there's still another hand

This is the one with which I fetch
water for your kitchen
write a thank-you note
strap-hang on a bus
I swing it vigorously as I walk
so it stays active defiant

That's when the other hand
crouches like a hare in a bush
or lies down in my childhood
somewhere between a ball and a rocking horse
In my youth it would clasp
the hand of a girl
but this swinging hand can't even
touch the other hand

It keeps on knocking
at the gates of cities offices houses
It's with this I do everything
It never gets tired never gives up
only when it's too much
the other hand protests
aching and trembling.

translated by Girdhar Rathi

दिनचर्या

कुछ ठोस उदाहरणों का हवाला देकर
हम कहते हैं यह दिन बीत गया
सुबह दरवाज़ा है हमारी आत्मा का
इसे हम खटखटाते हैं कामकाजी तरीक़े से

उठो और चल दो
अपनी दैनिक निराशा अर्जित करने के लिए

हम जानते हैं
धुआं ख़ून और चीख़ बहुत पहले से मौजूद हैं
इस सबकी छाप है हमारे विचारों पर
अपने विचारों से ज़्यादा दूर नहीं गये हैं हम

हम सड़क पर आते हैं
कविताओं-कहानियों की खोज में
हाथ बांधकर परस्पर बातचीत करते हैं
हमारी आस्था है इस तरह बातचीत करने में
तेज़ी से कमरे में टहलते हैं अख़बार पर झल्लाते हैं
अंत में हम कहते हैं भयानक है यह सब

हमने नहीं सोचा था मनुष्यता का भी एक ग़र्त है
हमने नहीं सोचा था अत्याचारी भी कहेगा
मेरा चेहरा मिलता है आदमी से
हम नहीं थे इस अपराध इस पागलपन में शामिल
सोचते हुए हम देखते हैं
समाज जा रहा है तेज़ी से रसातल

Daily Grind

Citing a few concrete instances
we say the day is done
Morning's a door to our soul
we knock at in a routine way

Get up and get going
to earn your daily ration of despair

We know it had all been there for a long time
smoke blood and shrieking
Their shadow falls on our thoughts
we have not ventured far
from our thoughts

We step onto the street
looking for poems and tales
we converse with folded hands
for we believe in such conversation
Briskly we pace in the room to and fro
and swear at newspapers
finally saying it's all too horrible

We never thought there would be an abyss
even in humanity
we never thought the tyrant one day
would compare his face
with that of a human
Thinking we were not privy
to this misdeed to this madness
we watch society slip
day after day
into the netherworld

बचा ले आये हैं हम रोटी में नमक बराबर जीवन
सलामत हैं हमारे सर चक्कर खाते हुए
आत्मा के दरवाज़े से गुज़रते हुए हम सोचते हैं
करुणा राहत उदारता के बारे में.

We have brought with us life
salvaged
though no more than a pinch of salt
our heads are still intact though dizzy
As we pass through the door of our soul
we reflect
on compassion succor magnanimity

translated by Girdhar Rathi

हम

अपना रास्ता चलते हुए
हम आपस में कहते हैं
संभलकर चलो
हमें चलना है कई साल

घर से निकलना है
घर में प्रवेश करना है
चींटी चाल चलते कभी हड़बड़ करते
बचे रहना है आंधी से
जो आने को है कभी भी
त्वचा हमारी दूर से भांप लेती है
हवा में ख़त्म होती नमी को

फूलों और भिखारियों को
पीछे छोड़ते हुए हम चलते हैं
रास्ते में बिखरे ख़ून को न देखते
रोते हुए बच्चे से कहते
चुप रहो चुप
अभी चलना है कई साल

ठीक से चलिए साहब
लड़खड़ाते आदमी से कहना चाहते हैं हम
दुनिया में फैल रही है थकान
हम देर तक बातचीत करते हैं सहमत होते हैं
तारों के नीचे लौटते हुए हम नहीं पूछते
कहां जाती होगी यह सड़क

जो जा रहे हैं उन्हें विदा करते
हम आपस में कहते हैं
संभलकर चलो
बचते हुए अपने शरीर की सिहरन से.

We

Walking our way
We say among ourselves
Walk carefully
We have to keep walking for several days

We have to leave our homes
And enter them again
Sometimes like ants and sometimes in great hurry
We have to protect ourselves from the hurricane
Which could arrive anytime
Our skin senses from a distance
The lessening moisture in the air

Leaving flowers and beggars behind
We walk on
Not looking at the blood spilled on the streets
To keep quiet
They have to walk for several years

Walk properly, sir,
We wish to tell the floundering man
A weariness spreads over the world
We talk late into the night
Agreeing among ourselves
Returning under the stars we do not ask
Where should this lead to ultimately

Bidding farewell to those who depart
We say among ourselves
Walk carefully
Avoid the shiver under your skin

translated by Girdhar Rathi

दिल्ली-2

सड़कों पर बसों में बैठकघरों में इतनी बड़ी भीड़ में
कोई नहीं कहता आज
मुझे निराला की कुछ पंक्तियां याद आयीं. कोई नहीं कहता
मैंने नागार्जुन को पढ़ा है.
कोई नहीं कहता किस तरह मरे मुक्तिबोध.

एक कहता है मैंने कर ली है ख़ूब तरक्क़ी. एक खुश है कि
उसे बस में मिल गयी है सीट. एक कहता है यह समाज
क्यों नहीं मानता मेरा हुक्म.एक देख चुका है
अपना पूरा भविष्य. एक कहता है
देखिए किस तरह बनाता हूं अपना रास्ता.

एक कहता है मैं हूँ ग़रीब. मेरे पास नहीं है
कोई और शब्द.

Delhi: 2

These days in streets buses living rooms
enormous crowds no one recalls
a single line of Nirala's. No one
avers he has read Nagarjun.
No one recounts how Muktibodh died.
No one wonders what sort of life it is.

One declaims he has made marked
progress. One demurs what did he need
now that he has a seat in
the bus. One asserts he has got the
blueprints for the future. One
excoriates why society would not
obey his command. One singsongs he's
making way by and by.

One says one is poor. One has no
word but that.

translated by Girdhar Rathi

पहाड़ पर लालटेन

जंगल में औरतें हैं
लकड़ियों के गट्ठर के नीचे बेहोश
जंगल में बच्चे हैं
असमय दफ़नाये जाते हए
जंगल में नंगे पैर चलते बूढ़े हैं
डरते-खांसते अंत में ग़ायब हो जाते हुए
जंगल में लगातार कुल्हाड़ियां चल रही हैं
जंगल में सोया है रक्त

धूप में तपती हुई चट्टानों के पीछे
वर्षों के आर्तनाद हैं
और थोड़ी-सी घास है बहुत प्राचीन
पानी में हिलती हुई
अगले मौसम के जबड़े तक पहुंचते पेड़
रातोंरात नंगे होते हैं
सूई की नोक जैसे सन्नाटे में
जली हुई धरती करवट लेती है
और एक विशाल चक्के की तरह घूमता है आसमान

जिसे तुम्हारे पूर्वज लाये थे यहां तक
वह पहाड़ दुख की तरह टूटता आता है हर साल
सारे वर्ष सारी सदियां
बर्फ़ की तरह जमती जाती हैं निःस्वप्न आंखों में
तुम्हारी आत्मा में
चूल्हों के पास पारिवारिक अंधकार में
बिखरे हैं तुम्हारे लाचार शब्द
अकाल में बटोरे गये दानों जैसे शब्द

दूर एक लालटेन जलती है पहाड़ पर
एक तेज़ आंख की तरह
टिमटिमाती धीरे-धीरे आग बनती हुई
देखो अपने गिरवी रखे हुए खेत
बिलखती स्त्रियों के उतारे गये गहने
देखो भूख से बाढ़ से महामारी से मरे हुए
सारे लोग उभर आये हैं चट्टानों से

Lantern on Mountain

In the jungle are women
Unconscious under bundles of wood
In the jungle are children
Buried before their time
In the jungle barefoot old men
Afraid and coughing disappear in the end
In the jungle blood has slept.

Behind the cliffs heated in the sun
The cries of centuries of pain
And just a little grass—quite ancient
Swaying in the water;
Trees reaching the jaws of the next season
Night after night become naked;
In the stillness like the point of a needle
The burning earth rolls on her side
And the sky revolves like a huge millstone.

The mountain your ancestors brought this far
Every year breaks more and more, like grief
All the years all the centuries
Freeze like ire in dreamless eyes
In your soul
In the domestic darkness of the hearth
Your helpless words are spread
Like grain gathered in a famine.

In the distance glows a lantern on a mountain
Like a luminous eye
Twinkling slowly becoming a fire—
Look at your mortgage filed,
The jewelry taken off sobbing women,
Look at all the people dead
From hunger, from flooding, from disease
Who've risen up on the cliffs

दोनों हाथों से बेशुमार बर्फ़ झाड़कर
अपनी भूख को देखो
जो एक मुस्तैद पंजे में बदल रही है
जंगल से लगातार एक दहाड़ आ रही है
और इच्छाएं दांत पैने कर रही हैं
पत्थरों पर.

Wiping away infinite snow with their hands,
Look at your own hunger
Becoming a quick claw;
From the jungle comes a constant roar
And desires sharpen their teeth
On the rocks.

translated by Robert Hueckstedt

थकान

शाम को सारी दुनिया को झाड़कर
बिस्तर पर
औंधा होकर अंत में
क्या बचता है कंधे पर बैठे दुख के अलावा
आत्मा पर फफूंद के अलावा क्या बचता है
अंत में

धीरे-धीरे दिनचर्या के नीचे दबा हुआ
अंधेरा ऊपर उठता है
पार्कों से आयी हुई हवा पार्कों में लौट जाती है
बच्चे घरों में बंद हो जाते हैं
दिन-भर देखी गयी स्त्रियां देर तक दिमाग़ में
गूंजकर सोने चली जाती हैं
एक तेज़ नदी की तरह सन्नाटा उतरता है आसमान से

रात जब निश्शब्द
हमारी छाती पर झुकी होती है
काले रंग की थकान बिस्तर पर चढ़ती है
मांसपेशियों के मोड़ लांघती है
काले रंग की थकान
आत्मा में से उठाती है अपना हाथ

ये वर्ष ख़ामोशी की तरह खड़े हैं
धुंध-भरे इन कमरों में नींद है
जिनमें अतीत है प्रज्ज्वलित मोमबत्तियों की तरह
इनकी छतों पर बर्फ़ जम चुकी है
सीटियां मारते किलकार करते
स्वप्न उन पर चलते हैं
ख़ून की लकीरें छोड़ते हुए

आधी रात रोशनी में
पेड़ चुपचाप पत्तियां गिरा रहे होते हैं
आधी रात पशुओं की वासना में
दबी धरती फैल रही होती है
आधी रात खंडहरों से राख उड़ती है
हमारी हड्डियों पर.

Exhaustion

In the evening, having shaken off the world,
Face down on the bed, in the end
What's left but misery riding one's shoulders
What's left in the end
But mold on the soul

Slowly, kept down by daily routine,
Darkness rises,
The park's breezes return to the parks,
The children are incarcerated at home,
The women watched all day
Reverberating late in the brain
Go off to sleep,
Like a roaring river
A hush descends from the sky
When night mutely
Crouches on my chest,
Black exhaustion climbs into bed
Negotiates the curve of muscles
Raises its hand from the abyss

The years stand like silence,
In them, in haze-filled rooms, is sleep,
The Past there is like burning candles,
On the Years' roofs ice has formed,
Over them walk whistling screaming dreams
Trailing lines of blood

In the light in the middle of the night
Trees quietly keep dropping their leaves,
In the minds of animals in the middle of the night
The constrained earth spreads out to infinity,
In the middle of the night
Ruin-risen ash falls
On my bones.

translated by Robert Hueckstedt

बच्चा

उसे याद था ठीक-ठीक कितने
खिलौने तोड़े उसने हर साल
कितनी बार रोया अकेला पड़ जाने पर
पत्थरों पर कितनी बार गिरा
और उठकर चल दिया घर की तरफ़
एक-एक कर सारे सपने उसे याद थे
जिनमें बच्चे ही बच्चे दिखते थे
उसे अपनी ओर आते हुए
हर चीज़ का स्वाद अलग-अलग
टिका रहता था उसकी जीभ पर

धीरे-धीरे वह बड़ा हुआ
और एकाएक बड़ा हो गया
अब वह हरदम हंसता था
उसे याद नहीं कितनी बार
सपनों की जगह जली हुई ज़मीन थी
जहां कभी-कभी सुनाई पड़ती थी
उसके मां-बाप के रोने की आवाज़.

A Child

He remembered exactly
Every year how many toys he broke
How many times he cried left alone
How many times he fell on the stones
And got up and ran fast for home;
He remembered every dream individually
In which only children appeared
Coming his way
The taste of each thing one by one
Rested on his tongue
Till the next one had come.

Gradually he became older,
And suddenly he was an adult.
Now he laughs
That he's forgotten how many times
The place of his dream
Was a land on fire
Where sometimes he could hear
His mother and father crying.

translated by Robert Hueckstedt

आख़िरी वारदात

जीभ लपलपाते दिन
मेरे सर से चले जाते हैं
और धूप मुझे कुछ और मूर्ख बनाकर
छोड़ देती है शहर के बीचों-बीच
एक अजीब-सी धुंध में
चौंककर मैं आंखें साफ़ करता हूं
शहर एक स्थायी बाढ़ में बहता चला जाता है
मुझे लकड़ी या पत्थर की तरह
किनारे फेंकता हुआ

मेरा चश्मा जो कि मुझे
उदास और रोबीला बनाता है
अक्सर मेरी आत्मा के अतल में
धंसा हुआ करकता है
रात को जब मैं सिगरेट बाले हुए
बिस्तर पर पड़ा होता हूं
मुझे अपने गले से
एक अश्लील घरघराहट सुनाई देती है
और मैं टटोलता हूं चेहरे पर उभरते
इच्छाओं के खुरदरे सींग

मैंने देखा है कई साल से
स्तब्ध लड़कियों को
जो दफ़्तरों से निकलकर
कटे हुए पौधों की तरह फैल जाती हैं
सड़कों पर कहीं न देखती हुईं
मैंने मकानों के पिछवाड़े से उठती हुई
भूख देखी है
तहस-नहस रात के कठघरे में चिल्लाते
कुछ पागलों को देखा है
और सुनी है झनझनाते दिमाग़ में
गूंजती हुई एक असमर्थ टाप

Final Incident

Flicking out their tongues the days
Slither past my head
And daylight makes me even duller
And leaves me in the middle of the city
In a peculiar haze.
I'm startled and clear my eyes,
The city drifts on in a perpetual flood
Tossing me to the side
Like a stone or piece of wood.

My glasses, often giving me
An indifferent and imposing air,
Plumb my bottomless soul and smash
At night when I light a cigarette
While lying on the bed;
An obscene wheeze
Rises from my throat
And I feel around
For jagged horns of desire
Taken root on my face.

For many years I've seen numb girls,
Like cut saplings,
Exit their offices and disperse
Looking at nothing on the streets;
I've seen hunger rising behind houses;
I've seen the insane screaming
In the ruined night's wooden cage;
And I've heard an insensible clopping of hooves
Resounding in my rattled brain.

एक आख़िरी वारदात के अंतर्गत
हर तरफ़ हरे पेड़ हिल रहे हैं
शहर में धूल जम रही है
लोग एक-दूसरे को धक्का देते
और आगे खिसक लेते हैं
अंधेरे में फूले पेट की एक औरत ऊंघती है
उसके तीन मरियल बच्चे
आपस में पिटते हैं
और मैं दोनों हाथ बांधता हुआ
बस-स्टॉप पर खड़ा होता हूं
जहां एक ताज़ा पोस्टर मेरी प्रतीक्षा में है
और एक अज्ञात चिड़िया
मेरी स्मृति में चहचहाने को आतुर है.

Within a final incident
Green trees are swaying all around
The dust is settling in the city
People elbow one another aside
And slip out ahead;
In the darkness a big-bellied woman is drowsy,
Her three sickly children
Beat each other
And I, hands clasped,
Stand at the bus stop
Where a fresh poster waits for me
And an unknown bird is
Eager to sing into my memory.

translated by Robert Hueckstedt

वापसी

बहुत बूढ़े होने पर भी आप अगर एक भूले-भटके बच्चे की तरह पर जायें तो वहां पिता मां या अन्य स्वजन होंगे जो ठीक बचपन में आपको पहचान लेंगे. वहीं कहीं आपकी कोई सच्ची प्रेमिका अजन्मी अपनी संतान के बाल काढ़ती वासना की रात को चादर की तरह बिछाती होगी. आप अगर जंगल की ओर जायें तो किसी शिकारी की तरह नहीं एक पेड़ की तरह जाना बेहतर होगा. एक बड़ा पेड़ आपको अपने भीतर छिपा लेगा. आपके चलने से हल्की-सी धूल उड़ेगी और धूप में देर तक चमकती रहेगी. आप अपने पत्तों को हिलाकर आवाज़ करेंगे तो वहां से हवा का बहना शुरू होगा. वहां कोई कहानी या उसका एक हिस्सा बचा हुआ होगा जिसके खंडहर में रहा जा सकता है. बारिश आपको खींच ले जायेगी और बर्फ़ वापस भेज देगी. कुछ दूर तक उन चीज़ों के पीछे चलना अच्छा होगा जिनके अर्थ समझ में नहीं आते. आप उन पुराने टूटे-फूटे आईनों में प्रवेश कर सकते हैं जो अब सिर्फ़ अपनी स्मृति में डूबे हुए हैं. शायद आप वहां कोई सपना देखें या आपके भीतर किसी धुंधली-सी चीज़ का जन्म हो और आप उस क्षण को फिर से पा लें जिसके पहले आप वह थे जो उसके बाद नहीं रहे.

Return

If you were to return home like a lost and long-forgotten child, then, though you had become quite old, your mother, father, or some other relative would recognize you as if you had never left. Your true love, combing out the hair of your unborn child, would spread it out like the sheet of your nuptial night. If you go to the jungle, better go as a tree than a hunter. A taller tree will hide you below it. From your tread a light dust will rise and twinkle in the sunlight. Shaking your leaves will make a sound that sets off the ripples of a breeze. A story will be there, or some preserved fragment of it, in the ruins of which you can live. Rain will pull you out; snow will send you back. It will be good to follow for some distance those things you do not understand. You will be able to enter into old, broken mirrors immersed only in their own memories. There you may see dreams, or something indistinct may be born within you, and you will experience again that moment before which you were what you did not remain.

translated by Robert Hueckstedt

सात दिन का सफ़र

पहले एक साफ़ धुली हुई चादर की तरह सोमवार प्रकट होता है
और उम्मीद बंधती है कि इस लंबे सफ़र में
कुछ नये सिरे से किया जा सकता है
हम रास्ते की दिक़्क़तों और उन्हें लांघने की इच्छा का ख़ाका बनाते हैं
मंगलवार एक चट्टान की तरह है
एक दुविधापूर्ण स्थिति जहां यह पता नहीं चलता
कि आगे कौन-सा मोड़ या कैसी ढलान है
और उसके लिए कितना उत्साह या सावधानी हम में होनी चाहिए
बुधवार के पारदर्शी कांच से हम कुछ दूर तक देख सकते हैं
कि कुछ भी उस तरह आसान नहीं है जैसा हम सोचते थे
और असमंजस अनिश्चय धुंधलका पहले की ही तरह है
अगला दिन गुरुवार एक पड़ाव की तरह लगता है
क्योंकि हम आधे रास्ते तक आ गये हैं
और जान सकते हैं कि हमारी ठीक-ठीक स्थिति क्या है
और शायद इसी में से कोई रास्ता निकलता है
इसी रास्ते पर शुक्रवार सांत्वना देता हुआ आता है
लेकिन यह तय है कि हम अभी तक कुछ नहीं कर पाये हैं
और अब समय बहुत कम रह गया है
और हमने किसी को चिट्ठी तक नहीं लिखी
इसी घबराहट में हम शनिवार में प्रवेश करते हैं
जो कि दरअसल एक तहख़ाना है जहां यह कहना कठिन है
कि हम चल रहे हैं या रुके हुए हैं
और जब कोई पूछता है कि क्या हाल हैं
तो हम कहते हैं बतलाने के लिए कुछ ख़ास नहीं है
अगली सुबह इतवार आ जाता है
यह छुट्टी का दिन है चीज़ें अपनी प्रागैतिहासिक
निश्चेष्टता में पड़ी हैं किताबें औंधी रखी हैं
चाय ठंढी हो चुकी है सामने गंदे कपड़ों का अंबार लगा है
और बाहर दरवाज़े पर किसी की धीमी दस्तक है.

The Seven-Day Journey

First, Monday flaps open like a freshly washed sheet
Hope snuggles up and says, This time
We can take a different approach
So we map out the problems along the way
And where the detours have to be
Tuesday's like a cliff
A blind either/or
Ahead do we turn or slide down the descent
And how much concentration and courage do we need?
Through Wednesday's binoculars we can see far ahead
It won't be as easy as Hope first had said
There he was, just as before,
Unsettling indefinite haze in the head.
Thursday's like an inn along the way
Half the distance we've already traveled
And now we know exactly where we stand
And perhaps in these difficult times, there may just be a way out
Coming along that very path Friday gives us patience
But it's clear that so far we've accomplished nothing
And now it's getting late
And we haven't even sent a postcard.
With that anxiety we enter Saturday
A subterranean space where it's difficult to tell
Whether we're moving or still
And when someone asks how I am
I say there's nothing worth telling.
The next morning Sunday comes
Day of rest and things
Assume their prehistoric immobility
Books lie open
The tea's gone cold
Over there the pile of dirty clothes
On the table the phone rings and rings
And on my door someone's hesitant knock.

translated by Robert Hueckstedt

बचपन की कविता

जैसे-जैसे हम बड़े होते हैं लगता है हम बचपन के बहुत क़रीब हैं. हम
अपने बचपन का अनुकरण करते हैं. ज़रा देर में तुनकते हैं और ज़रा देर
में ख़ुश हो उठते हैं. खिलौनों की दूकान के सामने देर तक खड़े रहते हैं.
जहां-जहां ताले लगे हैं हमारी उत्सुक आंखें जानना चाहती हैं कि वहां क्या
होगा. सुबह हम आश्चर्य से चारों ओर देखते हैं जैसे पहली बार देख रहे हों.

हम तुरंत अपने बचपन में पहुंचना चाहते हैं. लेकिन वहां का कोई नक़्शा
हमारे पास नहीं है. वह किसी पहेली जैसा बेहद उलझा हुआ रास्ता है अक्सर
धुएं से भरा हुआ. उसके अंत में एक गुफा है जहां एक राक्षस रहता है.
कभी-कभी वहां घर से भागा हुआ कोई लड़का छिपा होता है. वहां सख़्त
चट्टानें और कांच के टुकड़े हैं छोटे-छोटे पैरों से आसपास.

घर के लोग हमें बार-बार बुलाते हैं. हम उन्हें चिट्ठियां लिखते हैं आ रहे
हैं आ रहे हैं आयेंगे हम जल्दी.

A Poem on Childhood

The older I get the more a child I become. For a minute I'm angry and petulant, then I'm suddenly happy. In front of the toy store I stand for hours. My eager eyes want to know what's behind every lock. In the morning I look all around in amazement as if seeing the world for the first time.

I want to return to my childhood. But I have no map to get there. It is a riddle-like, complicated path. Often filled with smoke. At the end of it is a cave where a demon lives. Sometimes a boy hides there who's run away from home. Pieces of hard rock and glass beside his legs.

People from home keep shouting for me. I write them letters. I'm coming I'm coming I'll be home soon.

translated by Robert Hueckstedt

यहाँ थी वह नदी

जल्दी से वह पहुंचना चाहती थी
उस जगह जहां एक आदमी
उसके पानी में नहाने जा रहा था
एक नाव
लोगों का इंतज़ार कर रही थी
और पक्षियों की क़तार
आ रही थी पानी की खोज में

बचपन की उस नदी में
हम अपने चेहरे देखते थे हिलते हुए
उसके किनारे थे हमारे घर
हमेशा उफ़नती
अपने तटों और पत्थरों को प्यार करती
उस नदी से शुरू होते थे दिन
उसकी आवाज़
तमाम खिड़कियों पर सुनाई देती थी
लहरें दरवाज़ों को थपथपाती थीं
बुलाती हुईं लगातार

हमे याद है
यहां थी वह नदी इसी रेत में
जहां हमारे चेहरे हिलते थे
यहां थी वह नाव इंतज़ार करती हुई

अब वहां कुछ नहीं है
सिर्फ़ रात को जब लोग नींद में होते हैं
कभी-कभी एक आवाज़ सुनाई देती है रेत से.

This Is Where the River Was

There where a man was moving
towards its waters to bathe in,
a boat
lay waiting for people,
and a flock of birds
was approaching
in search of water.

In that river of childhood
we would see our faces, undulating.
Upon its banks stood our houses.
The days began from that river
which, surging without cease, loved
its banks and stones.
Its voice was heard at all windows.
The waves, their lure unbroken,
tapped on the doors.

We remember:
here was the river,
in these very sands,
where our faces rippled.
Here was the boat
that lay in wait.

Now nothing remains there.
Only at night when people are asleep,
sometimes a voice is heard
emanating from the sands.

translated by Sarabjeet Garcha

तुम्हारे भीतर

एक स्त्री के कारण तुम्हें मिल गया एक कोना
तुम्हारा भी हुआ इंतज़ार

एक स्त्री के कारण तुम्हें दिखा आकाश
और उसमें उड़ता चिड़ियों का संसार

एक स्त्री के कारण तुम बार-बार चकित हुए
तुम्हारी देह नहीं गयी बेकार

एक स्त्री के कारण तुम्हारा रास्ता अंधेरे में नहीं कटा
रोशनी दिखी इधर-उधर

एक स्त्री के कारण एक स्त्री
बची रही तुम्हारे भीतर.

Inside You

Because of a woman you could obtain a place.
You too were waited for.

Because of a woman you could see the sky
and, within it, the world of birds on the wing.

Because of a woman you were amazed again and again.
Your body didn't go in vain.

Because of a woman you didn't have to traverse
through the dark. You could glimpse light
here and there.

Because of a woman, a woman could remain
a woman within you.

translated by Sarabjeet Garcha

अनुपस्थिति

यहां बचपन में गिरी थी बर्फ़
पहाड़ पेड़ आंगन सीढ़ियों पर
उन पर चलते हुए हम रोज़ एक रास्ता बनाते थे

बाद में जब मैं बड़ा हुआ
देखा बर्फ़ को पिघलते हुए
कुछ देर चमकता रहा पानी
अंततः उसे उड़ा दिया धूप ने.

Absence

Snow had fallen here in my childhood,
on mountains trees courtyards stairs.
Traipsing along every day we'd make
a trail on it.

Later, when I grew up,
I saw the snow melting away.
The water kept shining for a while.
Finally the sun blew it away.

translated by Sarabjeet Garcha

प्रेम

वह कोई बहुत बड़ा मीर था
जिसने कहा था प्रेम एक भारी पत्थर है
कैसे उठेगा तुझ जैसे कमज़ोर से

मैने सोचा
इसे उठाऊं टुकड़ों-टुकड़ों में

पर तब वह कहां होगा प्रेम
वह तो होगगा एक हत्याकांड.

Love

It was an illustrious Mir
who said, *Love is an unwieldy rock.*
How would a weakling like you heave it up?

I thought,
Let me pick it up in pieces.

But then how would it be love any longer?
It'd be a massacre.

translated by Sarabjeet Garcha

कमरा

इस कमरे में सपने आते हैं
आदमी पहुंच जाता है
दस या बारह साल की उम्र में

यहां फ़र्श पर बारिश गिरती है
सोये हुओं पर बादल मंडराते हैं

रोज़ एक पहाड़ धीरे-धीरे
इस पर टूटता है
एक जंगल यहां अपने पत्ते गिराता है
एक नदी यहां का कुछ सामान
अपने साथ बहाकर ले जाती है

यहां देवता और मनुष्य दिखते हैं
नंगे पैर
फटे कपड़ों में घूमते
साथ-साथ घर छोड़ने की सोचते.

The Room

In this room dreams appear.
You get transported to
the age of ten, twelve.

Rain falls on the floor here,
clouds hover over those asleep.

Every day a mountain slowly
breaks apart over the room,
a forest sheds its leaves here,
a river washes away some
of this region's belongings.

Here god and man are for sale,
barefoot,
roving about in rags,
thinking of leaving
the house together.

translated by Sarabjeet Garcha

त्वचा

त्वचा ही इन दिनों दिखती है चारों ओर
त्वचामय बदन त्वचामय सामान
त्वचा का बना कुल जहान
टीवी रात-दिन दिखलाता है जिसके चलते-फिरते दृश्य
त्वचा पर न्योछावर सब कुछ
कई तरह के लेप उबटन झाग तौलिये आसमान से गिरते हुए
कमनीय त्वचा का आदान-प्रदान करते दिखते हैं स्त्री-पुरुष
प्रेम की एक परत का नाम है प्रेम
अध्यात्म की ख़ाल जैसा अध्यात्म
सतह ही सतह फैली है हर जगह उस पर नये-नये चमत्कार
एक सुंदर सतह के नीचे आसानी से छिप जाता है एक कुरूप विचार
एक दिव्य त्वचा पहनकर प्रकट होता है मुकुटधारी भगवान

यह कोई और ही त्वचा है
जो जीती-जागती-धड़कती देह में से नहीं उपजती उसकी सुंदरता बनकर
जो सांस नहीं लेती जिसके रोंये नहीं सिहरते
जिसे पीड़ा नहीं महसूस होती
यह कबीर की मुई ख़ाल नहीं है
जिसकी गहरी सांस लोहे को भस्म कर देती है
यह कोई और ही त्वचा है जो कोई पुकार नहीं सुनती
जिसे छूने पर रक्त नहीं उछलता हृदय नहीं पसीजता
सतह पर पड़ा रहता है दुख
झुर्रियों के समुद्र में विलीन होती जाती मोटी ख़ाल की एक नदी
अपने साथ बहाकर ले जाती है सुगंधमय प्रसाधन तौलिये उबटन
यही है हमारा त्वचामय समय यही है हमारा निवास
इसी पर नाचते हैं हमारे विचार
देखो एक रोगशोकजरामरणविहीन कविता की दशा
वह यहां त्वचा की तरह सूखती हुई पड़ी है.

Skin

only the skin is visible everywhere
dermal bodies dermal objects
all universe made of skin
whose roving and spinning images the TV
flashes night and day
everything devoted to the skin
many kinds of cream unguents foam towels
falling from the sky
men and women are seen bartering
desirable skin
love's the name of a layer of love
spirituality is like spirituality's crust
only periphery is spread out everywhere
new miracles being worked on it
beneath a beautiful surface an ugly
thought hides easily
the crowned god appears wearing
a divine skin

this is some other skin that doesn't sprout
out of a living wakeful pulsing body
becoming its beauty
that doesn't breathe
whose hair doesn't stand on end
that doesn't feel pain
this is not Kabir's dead skin
whose deep breath burns iron turning it into ash
this is some other skin that never hears when called out
that doesn't spout blood doesn't rend the heart when touched
sorrow lies on the surface
a river of thick skin disappearing into the sea of wrinkles
washes away fragrant toilets towels unguents
this is our skin-suffused time this is our abode
our thoughts dance upon it
look at a poetry devoid of disease grief decay death
it lies here drying up like skin.

translated by Sarabjeet Garcha

ऐसा समय

जिन्हें दिखता नहीं
उन्हें कोई रास्ता नहीं सूझता
जो लंगड़े हैं वे कहीं नहीं पहुंच पाते
जो बहरे हैं वे जीवन की आहट नहीं सुन पाते
बेघर कोई घर नहीं बनाते
जो पागल हैं वे जान नहीं पाते
कि उन्हें क्या चाहिए

यह ऐसा समय है
जब कोई हो जा सकता है अंधा लंगड़ा
बहरा बेघर पागल.

These Times

Those who can't see
cannot make out their way
Those who are crippled
cannot reach anywhere
Those who are deaf
cannot listen to life's footfalls
The homeless don't build a home
Those who are mad wouldn't know
what they want

These are such times
when anybody can turn blind crippled
deaf homeless mad.

translated by Sarabjeet Garcha

दिल्ली - एक

दस लोगों का परिवार मारुति डीलक्स में ठुंसा जा रहा था. दोस्त से गहन चर्चा में लीन चित्रकार सामने से आती बस देखकर सहसा लपक पड़ा. कोने में एक औरत अपने बच्चे को पीट रही थी. एक नौजवान खुले आम एक युवती से प्रेम करने का स्वांग करता था.

एक आदमी कुहनियों से अगल-बग़ल धक्के मारकर काफ़ी आगे निकल गया. कंप्यूटर के सामने बैठा दिल का मरीज़ सोचता था देश का इलाज़ कैसे करूं. आलीशान बाज़ार के पिछवाड़े एक वीर पुरुष रो रहा था जिसे वीरता की बीमारी थी. एक सफल आदमी सफलता के गुप्त रोग का शिकार था. एक प्रसिद्ध अत्याचारी विश्व पुस्तक मेले में हंसता हुआ घूम रहा था.

इस शहर में दिखाई देते हैं विचित्र लोग. उनके चहरे मेरे शत्रुओं से मिलते हैं. आरामदेह कारों में बैठकर वे जाते हैं इंदिरा गांधी अंतरराष्ट्रीय हवाई अड्डे की ओर.

Delhi: 1

A family of ten crammed into a Maruti Deluxe was cruising around. Sighting a bus coming from the opposite direction, a painter in deep conversation with a friend made a dash toward it. In a corner a woman was thrashing her child. A young man was openly wheedling a young woman.

A man jostled his way through and got far ahead. A heart patient facing the computer was thinking, *How do I cure the country?* At the rear of the plush market a brave man was crying; he was afflicted with the malady of bravery. A successful man had fallen prey to the secret disease of success. A famous tyrant, laughing, was wandering around at the World Book Fair.

I see bizarre people in this city. Their faces resemble the faces of my enemies. Lolling in luxury cars they go toward Indira Gandhi International Airport.

translated by Sarabjeet Garcha

बची हुई जगहें

रोज़ कुछ भूलता कुछ खोता रहता हूं
चश्मा कहां रख दिया है क़लम कहां खो गया है
अभी-अभी नीला रंग देखा था वह पता नहीं कहां चला गया
चिट्ठियों के जवाब देना कर्ज़ की क़िस्तें चुकाना भूल जाता हूं
दोस्तों को सलाम और विदा कहना याद नहीं रहता
अफ़सोस प्रकट करता हूं कि मेरे हाथ ऐसे कामों में उलझे रहे
जिनका मेरे दिमाग़ से कोई मेल नहीं था
कभी ऐसा भी हुआ जो कुछ भूला था उसका याद न रहना भूल गया

मां कहती थी उस जगह जाओ
जहां आख़िरी बार तुमने उन्हें देखा उतारा या रखा था
अमूमन मुझे वे चीज़ें फिर से मिल जाती थीं और मैं ख़ुश हो उठता
मां कहती थी चीज़ें जहां होती हैं
अपनी एक जगह बना लेती हैं और वह आसानी से मिटती नहीं
मां अब नही है सिर्फ़ उसकी जगह बची हुई है

चीज़ें खो जाती हैं लेकिन जगहें बनी रहती हैं
हम कहीं और चले जाते हैं अपने घरों लोगों अपने पानी और पेड़ों से दूर
मैं जहां से एक पत्थर की तरह खिसक कर चला आया
उस पहाड़ में भी एक छोटी-सी जगह बची होगी
इस बीच मेरा शहर एक विशालकाय बांध के पानी में डूब गया
उसके बदले वैसा ही एक और शहर उठा दिया गया
लेकिन मैंने कहा मेरा शहर अब एक ख़ालीपन है

घटनाएं विलीन हो जाती हैं
लेकिन जहां वे जगहें बनी रहती हैं जहां वे घटित हुई थीं
जमा होती जाती हैं साथ चलती हैं
याद दिलाती हुईं कि हम क्या भूल गये हैं
और हमने क्या खो दिया है.

The Places That Are Left

These days, I keep forgetting things, keep losing them,
I misplace my glasses, lose my pen,
a second ago, somewhere, I saw the color blue,
now I do not know where it has gone.
I forget answering letters, paying my debts,
I forget saying my hellos and goodbyes to friends,
regretting that my hands remain full with work
that has little to do with me,
sometimes, having forgotten a thing,
I cannot even remember forgetting it.

Mother used to tell me to go to those places
where I had last seen, taken off, or kept those things.
This way I usually found them and was thrilled.
Mother used to say that these things, wherever they are,
make a place of their own and do not let go easily.
Now Mother is no longer with me,
only her place is left.

Things get lost but their places remain,
moving with us all our lives.
We move elsewhere, leaving our homes, our people,
the water, the trees,
like a stone I had washed away from a mountain,
that mountain must still have a little place left.
Meanwhile, my city was submerged by a big dam,
they have made another city in its place
but I said this is not it, my city is now an empty feeling.

Things happen and then pass
but where they happened, those places add up,
those places move with me,
reminding me of all that I have forgotten
and of all that I have lost.

translated by Akhil Katyal

मैं चाहता हूं

मैं चाहता हूं कि स्पर्श बचा रहे
वह नहीं जो कंधे छीलता हुआ
आततायी की तरह गुज़रता है
बल्कि वह जो एक अनजानी यात्रा के बाद
धरती के किसी छोर पर पहुंचने जैसा होता है

मैं चाहता हूं स्वाद बचा रहे
मिठास और कड़वाहट से दूर
जो चीज़ों को खाता नहीं है
बल्कि उन्हें बचाये रखने की कोशिश का एक नाम है

एक सरल वाक्य बचाना मेरा उद्देश्य है
मसलन यह कि हम इंसान हैं
मैं चाहता हूं इस वाक्य की सचाई बची रहे
सड़क पर जो नारा सुनाई दे रहा है
वह बचा रहे अपने अर्थ के साथ

मैं चाहता हूं निराशा बची रहे
जो फिर से एक उम्मीद
पैदा करती है अपने लिए
शब्द बचे रहें
जो चिड़ियों की तरह कभी पकड़ में नहीं आते

प्रेम में बचकानापन बचा रहे
कवियों में बची रहे थोड़ी लज्जा.

I Wish

I wish that touch remained,
not the kind which, bruising shoulders,
passes like a tyrant,
but one which after a strange journey
is like reaching an edge of the earth.

I wish that taste remained
beyond sweetness or bitterness,
one which does not eat into things
but is instead like an effort
to save them.

I wish a simple sentence remained,
like, for example, we are human beings,
I wish the truth of this sentence remained—
the slogan I heard on the streets
may it remain, along with what it says.

I wish despair remained
that again gave
birth to hope, for us,
may words remain
which, like birds, cannot be caught.

I wish childishness remained in love,
some shame remained in poets.

translated by Akhil Katyal

चुंबन

चुंबनों का इतिहास मनुष्य जाति की ही तरह प्राचीन है लेकिन वह मशहूर या सबसे लंबे या सबसे संक्षिप्त चुंबनों के नीरस वर्णनों या विज्ञापनों से ज़्यादा कुछ नहीं है. चुंबन एक ऐसी घटना है जो इतिहास के बाहर होती है. एक बिल्कुल अवास्तविक संसार में स्त्री-पुरुष के दीप्त होंठ परस्पर इतने पास जा जाते हैं कि उनकी सिहरन भी सुनी जा सकती है. शरीर का तमाम रक्त होठों की ओर दौड़ रहा है सारे विचार होठों पर इकट्ठा हो चुके हैं एक नम हृदय होठों तक पहुंच गया है और आत्मा भी वहीं निवास करने लगी है. यह एक ऐसा क्षण है जब एक फूल खिलता है कोई छोटी-सी चिड़िया उड़ान भरती है कहीं तारे चमकते हैं पृथ्वी के नीचे के पानी बहने की आवाज़ आती है लेकिन प्रकृति की ये सहज चीज़ें अस्तित्व को कंपा देनेवाले तरीक़े से घटित होती है. अंततः रक्त पीछे लौटता है और हृदय उसे पूरे शरीर में भेजने की अपनी पुरानी भूमिका निभाने लगता है. विचार दिमाग़ में पुनः प्रवेश करते हैं और आत्मा ज़िंदगी के बियाबान में लौट जाती है. अब सब कुछ सामान्य है. हम एक आंधी या एक आग से बचकर आये हैं. हम जीवित हैं और इतिहास में लौट चुके हैं और राहत की एक गहरी सांस ले रहे हैं.

Kiss

The history of the kiss is as old as mankind but it is usually nothing more than dry descriptions or advertisements for the famous, or the longest or the shortest kisses. A kiss always happens outside history. In that false world, the incandescent lips of two people come so close to each other that you can hear them tremble. All the blood from the body runs to the lips, all thoughts already gather on the lips, softly the heart reaches there and the soul finds a home there. This is that moment when a flower blooms small bird takes flight stars shine somewhere from under the earth you hear the water flowing but each of these usual events occurs in a way that shakes the ground you stand on. At last, the blood returns and the heart resumes its old role of pushing it through the entire body. Thoughts come back to mind and the soul returns to the wilderness. Now everything is ordinary again. We have narrowly escaped a storm, or a fire. We are alive and have returned to history, and are heaving a sigh of relief.

translated by Akhil Katyal

न्यू आर्लींस में जैज़

शराब की जो बोतलें अमेरिका में भरी हुई दिखी थीं
वे यहां ख़ाली और टूटी हुई हैं
सड़कों के किनारे बिखरे हुए नुकीले कांच और पत्थर
जैज़ जैज़ जैज़ एक लंबी कठिन अछोर गली
दोनों तरफ़ गिलासों के जमघट उनमें शराब कांपती है
लोग उसमें अपनी तक़लीफ़ को रोटी की तरह डुबोकर खाते हैं
गोरा होटल का मैनेजर कहता है उधर मत जाइए
वहां बहुत ज़्यादा अपराध हैं
यहां के दूरिस्त निर्देशों को ग़ौर से पढ़िए
अमेरिका के पांच सबसे हिंसक शहरों में है न्यू आर्लींस

चंद्रमा अपने सारे काले बेटे यहां भेज देता है
रात अपनी तमाम काली बेटियां यहां भेज देती है
यहां तारे टूट कर गिरते हैं और मनुष्य बन जाते हैं
जैज़ जैज़ जैज़ नशे की एक नदी है मिसीसिपी
फ़्रेंच क्वार्टर में तीन सौ साल पहले आये थे ग़ुलाम
अफ़्रीक़ा से भैंसों की फ़ौज¹ की तरह लाये हुए
जैसे ही कोड़ों की मार कुछ कम होती
वे फिर से करने लगते गाने और नाचने का अपना प्रिय काम
उन्हें हुक्म दिया जाता मेज़ पर नहीं रसोईघरों में खाओ²
वे हंसते हुए जाते खाते और नाचते
एक चतुर क्रूर सभ्यता के लिए उन पर शासन करना कितना कठिन

उनके लिए बने सारे नियम और वे तोड़ते रहे सारे नियम
आते और जाते हैं कितने ही अत्याचारी
फ़्रांसीस स्पानी अमेरिकी इंसानों के ख़रीदार
समुद्र से उठते हुए कितने ही तूफ़ान
हरिकेन बेट्सी रीटा कैटरीना
तब भी प्रेम की तलाश ख़त्म नहीं होती इस दुनिया में
जहां हर चीज़ पर डॉलर में लिखी हुई है उसकी क़ीमत

जब क्लैरिनेट के रंध्रों से अंधेरा बह रहा था
ट्रंपेट के गले से रुंधी हुई कोई याद बाहर आ रही थी
जब सैक्सोफ़ोन के स्वर नदी के ऊपर घुमड़ रहे थे
जब एक ट्रॉंबोन इस शहर के दिल की तरह चमक रहा था

New Orleans Jazz

The beer bottles I see everywhere in America
are also here, but empty,
and broken, on the roadside are
shards of glass and stones—Jazz, jazz,
jazz, a long difficult way,
on both sides are swarms of glasses, in them
beer, trembling,
folks dip their troubles, like bread, in them.
The white hotel manager says:
"I'd avoid that side, if I were you,
there's a lot of crime there,
if I were you, I'd read those tourist notices carefully,
do you know, in America,
New Orleans is among the five most violent cities."

The moon sends all its black sons here
the night sends all its black daughters here,
here the falling stars become men and women—Jazz,
jazz, jazz, you can get drunk on Mississippi.
In the French Quarter, the slaves came three hundred years back,
herded like an army of buffaloes from Africa,[1] and
whenever the whips rested
the songs started, the dance broke out—
the order, always, was to "Eat in the kitchen,"[2]
they went laughing, ate,
then danced—how difficult it is to rule over people,
even if you are a cunning, cruel civilization.

There were always rules,
they were always breaking rules—
so many tyrants came and went,
French, Spanish, American buyers and sellers of people,
so many storms rose from the sea—
Hurricane Betsy Rita Katrina—
despite them, they are still looking for love in this world,
despite the tags that are still hanging on things.

मुझे दिखा एक मनुष्य काला वह ब्रेड खा रहा था
वह हंस रहा था बढ़ रहा था मेरी तरफ हाथ मिलाने के लिए
उसके मुंह में हंसी तारों जैसी चमकती थी
उसे बुलाती हुई दूर से आयी एक स्ट्रीटकार
उसका नाम था डिज़ायर[3]
दूर एक होटल में टूरिस्टों का इंतज़ार कर रहा था
डरा हुआ गोरा मैनेजर.

---

1. अश्वेत ब्लू गीत 'बफैलो सोल्जर कॉट इन अफ्रीका' का संदर्भ
2. प्रसिद्ध अमेरिकी अश्वेत कवि लैंग्स्टन ह्यूज़ की एक कविता पंक्ति
3. टेनेसी विलियम्स का प्रसिद्ध नाटक अ स्ट्रीटकार वेम्ड डिज़ायर. इस नाम की ट्राम अब भी न्यू आर्लींस में चलती है

When the dark was
flowing out from the clarinet keys, when
that parched memory was making its way out
the trumpet's full throat, when the saxophone's notes were
crowding on the river, then, a trombone
was so bright as if it was the heart of a city—
then, I saw that man, black, eating bread,
he was smiling and coming to shake my hands,
smiling, like stars—
and from faraway, a Streetcar was calling after him
its name was Desire,[3]
and faraway, a white hotel manager, afraid,
was waiting for the tourists.

---

1. Reference to a blues song, "Buffalo soldier caught in Africa."
2. Reference to well-known American poet Langston Hughes's poem "I,
   Too."
3. Tennessee Williams' play *A Streetcar Named Desire*. This tram still plies
   in New Orleans.

translated by Akhil Katyal

संगतकार

मुख्य गायक के चट्टान जैसे भारी स्वर का साथ देती
वह आवाज़ सुंदर कमज़ोर कांपती हुई थी
वह मुख्य गायक का छोटा भाई है
या उसका शिष्य
या पैदल चलकर सीखने आनेवाला दूर का कोई रिश्तेदार
मुख्य गायक की गरज में
वह अपनी गूंज मिलाता आया है प्राचीन काल से
गायक जब अंतरे की जटिल तानों के जंगल में
खो चुका होता है
या अपने ही सरगम को लांघकर
चला जाता है भटकता हुआ एक अनहद में
तब संगतकार ही स्थायी को संभाले रहता है
जैसे समेटता हो मुख्य गायक का पीछे छूटा हुआ सामान
जैसे उसे याद दिलाता हो उसका बचपन
जब वह नौसिखिया था

तारसप्तक में जब बैठने लगता है उसका गला
प्रेरणा साथ छोड़ती हुई उत्साह अस्त होता हुआ
आवाज़ से राख जैसा कुछ गिरता हुआ
तभी मुख्य गायक हो ढाढ़स बंधाता
कहीं से चला आता है संगतकार का स्वर
कभी-कभी वह यों ही दे देता है उसका साथ
यह बताने के लिए कि वह अकेला नहीं है
और यह कि फिर से गाया जा सकता है
गाया जा चुका राग
और उसकी आवाज़ में जो एक हिचक साफ़ सुनाई देती है
यों अपने स्वर को ऊंचा न उठाने की जो कोशिश है
उसे विफलता नहीं
उसकी मनुष्यता समझा जाना चाहिए.

The Accompanist

Supporting the heavy monolith of the main singer's voice
His own was graceful, thin and quavering.
He is the singer's younger brother
Or a pupil
Or a distant relative who comes on foot to learn.
Since long ago
The resonance of his voice has echoed
The sonority of his master's;
And when the singer's lost his way
In the tangled jungle of melodic uplands
Or strays into the void of unstruck sound
Beyond the further reaches of the scale
It's the accompanist who holds the steady theme,
Gathering up the things the singer left behind,
Reminding him of childhood days
When he was a novice.

When the singer's voice gives way in the higher register,
Inspiration deserting him and fervor waning,
An ashiness shedding from his voice
Then the accompanist's tones emerge to blend with his;
Or it may be that he joins in simply
To show the singer that he's not alone
And that the song that's sung and done
Can be sung anew once more
And that the audible faltering in his voice
Or his willful avoidance of the higher notes
Is evidence not of ineffectuality
But of humanity.

translated by Rupert Snell

पिता की तस्वीर

पिता की छोटी-छोटी बहुत-सी तस्वीरें
पूरे घर में बिखरी हैं
उनकी आंखों में कोई पारदर्शी चीज़
साफ़ चमकती है
वह अच्छाई है या साहस
तस्वीर में पिता खांसते नहीं
व्याकुल नहीं होते
उनके हाथ-पैर में दर्द नहीं होता
वे झुकते नहीं समझौते नहीं करते

एक दिन पिता अपनी तस्वीर की बग़ल में
खड़े हो जाते हैं और समझाने लगते हैं
जैसे अध्यापक बच्चों को
एक नक़्शे के बारे में बताता है
पिता कहते हैं मैं अपनी तस्वीर जैसा नहीं रहा
लेकिन मैंने जो नये कमरे जोड़े हैं
इस पुराने मकान में उन्हें तुम ले लो
मेरी अच्छाई ले लो उन बुराइयों से जूझने के लिए
जो तुम्हें रास्ते में मिलेंगी
मेरी नींद मत लो मेरे सपने लो

मैं हूं कि चिंता करता हूं व्याकुल होता हूं
झुकता हूं समझौते करता हूं
हाथ-पैर में दर्द से कराहता हूं
पिता की तरह खांसता हूं
देर तक पिता की तस्वीर देखता हूं.

A Picture of Father

There are lots of little pictures of Father
Scattered throughout the house
His eyes sparkle brightly
With something far-seeing
Goodness or courage ·
In the picture Father doesn't cough
He's not agitated
His hands and legs don't ache
He does not stoop or compromise

One day Father stands next to his picture
And begins explaining
Just as a teacher shows a map to his pupils
Father says I'm not like my picture
But the new rooms I've added
In this old house, you take them
Take my goodness to battle against those evils
That you'll meet along the way
Don't take my sleep take my dreams

It's me who's worried who is agitated
I stoop and compromise
I groan with the pain in my hands and feet
I cough like Father
I look at Father's picture for a long time.

translated by Rupert Snell

मां की तस्वीर

घर में मां की कोई तस्वीर नहीं
जब भी तस्वीर खिंचवाने का मौक़ा आता है
मां घर में खोयी हुई किसी चीज़ को ढूंढ़ रही होती है
या लकड़ी घास और पानी लेने गयी होती है
जंगल में उसे एक बार बाघ भी मिला
लेकिन वह डरी नहीं
उसने बाघ को भगाया घास काटी घर आकर
आग जलायी और सबके लिए खाना पकाया

मैं कभी घास या लकड़ी लाने जंगल नहीं गया
कभी आग नहीं जलायी
मैं अक्सर एक ज़माने से चली आ रही
पुरानी नक्क़ाशीदार कुर्सी पर बैठा रहा
जिस पर बैठकर तस्वीरें खिंचवाई जाती हैं
मां के चेहरे पर मुझे दिखाई देती है
एक जंगल की तस्वीर लकड़ी घास और
पानी की तस्वीर खोयी हुई एक चीज़ की तस्वीर.

A Picture of Mother

There's no picture of Mother in the house
Whenever there's a chance of having pictures taken
Mother is looking for something that's been misplaced
Or has gone for wood or grass or water
Several times she encountered a tiger in the jungle
But she wasn't afraid
She chased the tiger away cut grass and came home
Lit the fire and cooked for everyone

I never went to the jungle for grass or wood
Never lit the fire
I mostly just sat on the old carved chair
That has been used for taking pictures for ages
In Mother's face I see a picture of a jungle
A picture of wood grass and water a picture
Of something that's been misplaced

translated by Rupert Snell

अपनी तस्वीर

यह एक तस्वीर है
जिसमें थोड़ा-सा साहस झलकता है
और ग़रीबी ढंकी हुई दिखाई देती है
उजाले में खिंची इस तस्वीर के पीछे
इसका अंधेरा छिपा हुआ है

इस चेहरे की शांति
बेचैनी का एक मुखौटा है
करुणा और क्रूरता परस्पर घुलेमिले हैं
थोड़ा-सा गर्व गहरी शर्म में डूबा है
लड़ने की उम्र जबकि बिना लड़े बीत रही है
इसमें किसी युद्ध से लौटने की यातना है
और ये वे आंखें हैं
जो बताती हैं कि प्रेम जिस पर सारी चीज़ें टिकी हैं
कितना कम होता जा रहा है

आत्ममुग्धता और मसख़री के बीच
कई तस्वीरों की एक तस्वीर
जिसे मैं बार-बार खिंचवाता हूं
एक बेहतर तस्वीर खिंचने की
निरर्थक-सी उम्मीद में.

A Picture of Myself

This is a picture
In which a little courage gleams
And poverty appears concealed
Its darkness lurks
Behind the brightness the picture was taken in

The composure of this face
Is a mask for unease
Compassion and cruelty mingle here
A little pride is sunk deep in shame
And though the age for fighting passes unengaged
It bears the anguish of one returned from war
And these are the eyes which tell that love on which all things
    depend
Is growing less with every day

Between self-entrancement and buffoonery
One picture amongst many
Which I have taken over and over
In the vain hope of an improvement.

translated by Rupert Snell

गुणानंद पथिक

एक झलक में ही दिख जाता था गुणानंद पथिक का पूरा जीवन
कितने ही लोगों ने देखा होगा उन्हें
खंडहर हो रहे टिहरी क़स्बे की मुख्य सड़क पर
बस अड्डे की भीड़ में स्वरों की एक लहर की तरह प्रवेश करते हुए
गले से लटकता था पुराना हारमोनियम
और कंधे पर झोले में स्वरचित गीतों की पुस्तिकाएं
पहले चार आने और फिर पचास पैसे में एक
गुणानंद पथिक गाते थे पहाड़ को बदलने का गीत
गांव-गांव की दीदियों-भुलियों से कहते जागो जल्दी जाओ
तुमसे ही जायेंगे निठल्ले पहाड़
यह बात लिख लो यह गीत सुन लो
क्यों ग़रीब के घर कंटीली घास की भी किल्लत है
कैसे अमीर के घर सजे हैं रात-दिन पकवान
गुणानंद पथिक को सुनते लोग टॉफ़ी लेमनजूस भूलकर
ख़रीद लेते गीतों की किताब
उसे पढ़ते हुए जाते बस में बैठ घर की ओर

स्त्रियां जो गाती हैं उन्हीं धुनों पर
गुणानंद पथिक ने बनाये अपने नये गीत
जैसे पुरानी चीज़ को नया बनाकर लौटाने में हो रचना का आनंद
कइयों ने सीखा उनसे संगीत का पहला पाठ
रामलीलाओं में अलग से सुनाई देती उनकी बहरे तवील
लोग पहचान जाते बजा रहा है संगीत का वह कारीगर
जो सिर्फ़ सुनाता नहीं बदल भी देता है राग को
उनके गायन से ही शुरू होते थे कम्युनिस्ट पार्टी के जलसे तमाम
देहरादून टिहरी उत्तरकाशी पौड़ी तक
सफ़र में रहता था उनका छोटा-सा स्वप्न

Gunanand Pathik

In just a glance one could fathom
the whole life of Gunanand Pathik
Many must have seen him on the main road
of the decaying Tehri town, entering
the bus stand in a wave of musical notes
The old harmonium hung from his neck
pamphlets of his songs in his shoulder bag
that he sold first for a quarter of a rupee
and later for a half.
Gunanand Pathik used to sing songs spelling
change for the mountains
calling out to the village folk to wake up
for with them would awaken the still mountains
he would sing songs that told the difference
between the rich and the poor
Listening to him
people would forget the toffees and lemon drops
buy his book of songs and read it
on the bus journey back home.

Gunanand Pathik had composed his songs
to the tunes of the women's folk songs
as though all joy lay in changing the old into the new
Many learned from him their first lesson of music
His voice was heard at the Ramlila
and people would know that these notes were
made by their musical craftsman
who knew not just to sing a raga
but even change it.
With his songs began all the Communist Party rallies
from Dehradun to Rehri to Pauri
traveled his little dream always.

गुणानंद पथिक जान नहीं पाये उनके जीते जी बदल रहा था कुछ
या बदलते-बदलते रह गया था कुछ
कई तरह के नये बाजे बजे पहाड़ में
पैसे की आवाज़ आने लगी जगह-जगह सुनाई दिया व्यवसाय का हॉर्न
गीतों की किताब से ज़्यादा बड़े हो गये पचास पैसे
कम्युनिस्ट पार्टी के पास भी आये इस बीच कई लाउडस्पीरकर
टिहरी में भागीरथी पर शुरू हुआ एक बड़ा बांध
गुणानंद गाते रहे वहा पुराना गीत
यही थी उनके जीवन की आख़िरी झलक
फिर बैठने लगी उनकी आवाज़
मंद हो चला सुरीला वाद्य
भूलने लगे वे अपने रचे गीत
बचे-खुचे कम्युनिस्ट सोचते ही रहे
एक दिन हो पथिकजी का बड़ा-सा सार्वजनिक अभिनंदन
तभी हारमोनियम छोड़कर गये गुणानंद पथिक अज्ञात के पथ पर
पहाड़ का लोकगीत बनकर.

He knew not that something was changing around him
or that something had refused to change
Many new musical instruments resounded
in the mountains
Money was making its own music and
half a rupee became more powerful than
the book of songs
the Communist Party got big loudspeakers
A dam came up on the Bhagirathi in Tehri
Gunanand kept singing the old song
This was the last glimpse of his life
then his voice started growing faint
the notes of the musical instrument were lost
he started forgetting the songs
he himself had written and composed
The leftover Communists kept planning
a big reception to honor him
But Gunanand Pathik had given up his harmonium by then
and people had forgotten him like they forget a folk song.

translated by Nirupama Dutt

दो कवियों की कथा

(शमशेर और मुक्तिबोध की स्मृति में)

प्रेम के सबसे सघन कवि को प्रेम नहीं मिला
उसके सामने दूध रोटी दवा का हिसाब था
जिसे यह कभी समझ नहीं पाता
दुनिया आईनों से भरी हुई थी जिन्हें वह स्याही की तरह
अपने अंतर्जल में घोलता रहा
मनुष्य की भाषाएं तमाम बोली कबूतरों की
उसकी तड़प को उठाने में असमर्थ थीं
वह बहता रहा प्यास के पहाड़ों पर सुंदरता का प्रपात

यातना के सबसे बीहड़ कवि को यातना ही मिली
कड़ी मारें और एक से एक दुःस्वप्न
वही था प्रेम के कवि का एक सच्चा दोस्त
वह एक जंगल की तरह था बार-बार अपने पत्ते गिराता हुआ
अपने शब्दों को काटता
उसे चौराहे ही मिले जीवन में भागता रहा दम छोड़
जिन्होंने संसार में प्रेम नष्ट किया यातना पैदा की
उसने देखे रात में उनके जगमग जुलूस
इन दिनों वे दिन में भी जगह-जगह निकलते दिखते हैं

यातना का कवि जल्दी ही इस संसार से चला गया
तब प्रेम के कवि ने सोचा मुझे रहना चाहिए यहां कुछ दिन और
अंततः प्रेम ही है यातना का प्रतिकार
अन्याय का प्रतिशोध
फिर वह अकेला झेलता रहा सारी यातना रह सका जितनी देर.

Tale of Two Poets

The poet of great love didn't get love
in front of him lay an account of
milk, bread, medicines
that he never could quite understand
The world full of mirrors, he kept
diluting like ink into the liquid depths
of his inner world
searching for a touch or a medium
to take him across and yonder
But all the human languages and
all the cooing of the pigeons
could not quell his anguish
He just kept showering
beauteous waterfalls
on the mountains of thirst.

The poet of torment was tormented
over and again
horrendous tortures,
nightmares matchless
He remained the one friend of the poet of love
He lived like a forest often chopping his own words
Crossroads were his lot and he ran to flee them
At nightfall he witnessed the flittering processions
of those who had destroyed love and nursed torment
These days, such processions are taken out
even in the light of the day

The poet of torment departed early from the world
The poet of love thought that
he should live on for some time more
As love is the only answer to torment
The only reprisal to injustice
And then he alone endured all the torment
as long as he could.

translated by Nirupama Dutt

घर का रास्ता

कई बार मैंने कोशिश की
इस बाढ़ में से अपना एक हाथ निकालने की
कई बार भरोसा हुआ
कई बार दिखा यह है अंत

मैं कहना चाहता था
एक या दो मालूमी शब्द
जिन पर फ़िलहाल विश्वास किया जा सके
जो सबसे ज़रूरी हों फ़िलहाल

मैं चाहता था
एक तस्वीर के बारे में बतलाना
जो कुछ देर क़रीब-क़रीब सच हो
जो टंगी रहे चेहरों और
दृश्यों के मिटने के बाद कुछ देर

मैं एक पहाड़ का
वर्णन करना चाहता था
जिस पर चढ़ने की मैंने कोशिश की
जो लगातार गिराता था धूल और कंकड़
रहा होगा वह भूख का पहाड़

मैं एक लापता लड़के का
ब्योरा देना चाहता था
जो कहीं ग़ुस्से से खाता होगा रोटी
देखता होगा अपनी चोटों के निशान
अपने को कोसता
कहता हुआ चला जाऊंगा घर

मैं अपनी उदासी के लिए
क्षमा नहीं मांगना चाहता था
मैं नहीं चाहता था मामूली
इच्छाओं को चेहरे पर ले आना
मैं भूल नहीं जाना चाहता था
अपने घर का रास्ता.

The Way Home

I tried several times
to raise my hand above this flood
Several times I had hopes
At times I saw this was the end

I'd only wanted to say
one or two ordinary words
that could be depended on
for the time being
that would be essential
at least for the moment

I'd only wanted
to describe a picture
that would be almost true
for a while
that would hang there
after the faces and landscapes had faded

I wanted to describe a mountain
one I tried to climb once
that sent down a shower of dirt and pebbles
Could it have been a mountain of hunger

I wanted to give details
of a missing boy
who might be eating bread somewhere in anger
looking at his scars
cursing himself
saying I will go back home

I did not want to apologize
for my despair
I did not want my simple desires
to show on my face
I did not ever want to forget
the way back home.

translated by Vishnu Khare

सोने से पहले

सोने से पहले मैं सुबह के अख़बार समेटता हूं
दिन भर की सुर्ख़ियां परे खिसका देता हूं
मैं अत्याचारी तारीख़ों और हत्यारे दिनों को याद नहीं रखना चाहता
मैं नहीं जानना चाहता कितना रक्त बहाकर बनाये जा रहे हैं राष्ट्र
मैं वे तमाम तस्वीरें औंधी कर देता हूं
जिनमें एक पुल ढह रहा है कुछ सिसकियां उठ रही हैं
एक चेहरा जान बख़्श देने की भीख मांग रहा है
एक आदमी कुर्सी पर बैठा अट्टहास कर रहा है

क्या रात भर मुझे एक तानाशाह घूरता रहेगा
रात भर चलते हुए मुझे दिखेंगे घरों से बेदख़ल
एक अज्ञात उजाड़ की ओर जाते परिवार
क्या रात भर मेरा दम घोटता रहेगा धरढ़ी का बढ़ता हुआ तापमान
दिमाग़ में दस्तक देता रहेगा बाज़ार
सोने से पहले मैं किताबें बंद कर देता हूं
जिनमें पेड़ पहाड़ मकान मनुष्य सब काले-सफ़ेद अवसाद में डूबे हैं
और प्रेम एक उजड़े हुए घोंसले की तरह दिखाई देता है

सोने से पहले मैं तमाम भयानक दृश्यों को बाहर खदेड़ता हूं
और खिड़कियां बंद कर देता हूं
सिगरेट बुझाता हूं चप्पलें पलंग के नीचे खिसका देता हूं
सोने से पहले मैं एक गिलास पानी पीता हूं
और कहता हूं पानी तुम बचे रहना
एक गहरी सांस लेता हूं
और कहता हूं हवा तुम यहां रहो
मेरे फेफड़ों और दीवारों के बीच
सोने से पहले मैं कहता हूं
नींद मुझे दो एक ठीक-ठाक स्वप्न.

Before Going to Sleep

Before going to sleep I collect the morning papers
And push away the day's headlines
I don't like to remember the dates of killing and tyranny
I don't want to know how much bloodshed nations are making
I turn over the pictures
A bridge is collapsing lamentation is rising
A face begging for its lifeline
A man sitting on a chair roaring in laughter

All night will a despot keep staring at me
All night shall I keep seeing displaced people roaming
Moving towards some unknown arid land
All night will my breath suffocate due to earth's rising
    temperature
Will a bazaar keep knocking at my head
Before going to sleep I close my books
Where trees hills buildings people are all drowned in black-n-
    white sorrow
And love looks like a disheveled nest

Before going to sleep I drive all scary images away
And close the windows
Put out my cigarette slide my slippers under the bed
Before going to sleep I drink a glass of water
And say water you remain around
I take a deep breath
And say air stay here between my lungs and these walls
Before going to sleep I say
Sleep give me at least a nice enough dream.

translated by Sudeep Sen

छुओ

उन चीज़ों को छुओ जो तुम्हारे सामने मेज़ पर रखी हैं
घड़ी क़लमदान एक पुरानी चिट्ठी
बुद्ध की प्रतिमा बेटॉल्ट ब्रेश्ट और चे गेवारा की तस्वीरें
दराज़ खोलकर उसकी पुरानी उदासी को छुओ
शब्दों की अंगुलियों से एक ख़ाली काग़ज़ को छुओ
वन गॉग की पेंटिंग के स्थिर जल को एक कंकड़ की तरह छुओ
जो उसमें जीवन की हलचल शुरू कर देता है।
अपने माथे को छुओ
और देर तक उसे थामे रहने में शर्म महसूस मत करो
छूने के लिए ज़रूरी नहीं कोई बिलकुल पास में बैठा हो
बहुत दूर से भी छूना संभव है
उस चिड़िया की तरह दूर से ही जो अपने अंडों को सेती रहती है

कृपया छुएं नहीं या छूना मना है जैसे वाक्यों पर विश्वास मत करो
यह लंबे समय से चला आ रहा एक षड्यंत्र है
तमाम धर्मगुरु ध्वजा-पताका-मुकुट-उत्तरीयधारी
बमबाज़ जंगख़ोर सबको एक दूसरे से दूर रखने के पक्ष में हैं
वे जितनी गंदगी जितना मलबा उगलते हैं
उसे छूकर ही साफ़ किया जा सकता है
इसलिए भी छुओ भले ही इससे चीज़ें उलट-पुलट हो जायें

इस तरह मत छुओ जैसे भगवान महंत मठाधीश भक्त चेले
एक दूसरे के सर और पैर छूते हैं
बल्कि ऐसे छुओ जैसे
लंबी घासें चांद-तारों को छूने-छूने को होती हैं2
अपने भीतर जाओ और एक नमी को छुओ
देखो वह बची हुई है या नहीं इस निर्मम समय में.

---

1. जापानी फ़िल्मकार अकीरा कुरोसावा की फ़िल्म 'ड्रीम्स'' का एक अंश
2. शमशेर बहादुर सिंह की एक कविता पंक्ति

Touch

Touch the things that are kept on the table in front of you
Clock pen-stand an old letter
Idol of Buddha Bertolt Brecht and Che Guevara's photos
Open the drawer and touch its old sadness
Touch a blank sheet of paper with the words' fingers
Touch like a pebble the still water of a Van Gogh painting
Starting life's hullabaloo[1] in it
Touch your forehead and hold it for a long while without feeling
    shame
To touch it isn't necessary for someone to sit close
From very far it is possible to touch even
Like a bird from a distance who keeps her eggs protected

"Please do not touch" or "Touching is prohibited" don't believe in
    such phrases
These are long-running conspiracies
Religious gurus holding flags wearing crowns and shawls
Bomb-throwers, war-raisers indulge in for keeping us apart
The more dirt the more waste they spit
Only by touch can they be cleansed
Touch you must even though it turns things topsy-turvy

Don't touch the way gods priests bigots devotees disciples
Touch each other's feet and heads
Rather touch the way the tall grass appears to caress the moon
    and stars[2]
Go inward feel the moist spot touch
See if it still remains there or not in these ruthless times.

---

1. Reference to the Japanese filmmaker Akira Kurosawa's film on Van Gogh.
2. Reference to a poem by the major Hindi poet Shamsher Bahadur Singh.

translated by Sudeep Sen

यह नंबर मौजूद नहीं

दिस नंबर डज़ नॉट एग्ज़िस्ट
जहां भी जाता हूं जो भी फ़ोन मिलाता हूं
अकसर एक बेगानी-सी आवाज़ सुनाई देती है
दिस नंबर डज़ नॉट एग्ज़िस्ट यह नंबर मौजूद नहीं है
कुछ समय पहले इस पर मिला करते थे बहुत-से लोग
कहते आ जाओ हम तुम्हें पहचानते हैं
इस अंतरिक्ष में तुम्हारे लिए भी बना दी गयी है एक जगह

लेकिन अब वह नंबर मौजूद नहीं है वह कोई पहले का नंबर था
उन पुराने पतों पर बहुत कम लोग बचे हुए हैं
जहां आहट पाते ही दरवाज़े खुल जाते थे
अब घंटी बजाकर कुछ देर सहमे हुए बाहर खड़े रहना पड़ता है
और आख़िरकार जब कोई प्रकट होता है
तो मुमकिन है उसका हुलिया बदला हुआ हो
या वह कह दे मैं वह नहीं हूं जिससे तुम बात करते थे
यह वह नंबर नहीं है जिस पर तुम सुनाते थे अपनी तकलीफ़

जहां भी जाता हूं देखता हूं बदल गये हैं नंबर नक़्शे चेहरे
नाबदानों में पड़ी हुई मिलती हैं पुरानी डायरियां
उनके नाम धीरे-धीरे पानी में घुलते हुए
अब दूसरे नंबर मौजूद हैं पहले से कहीं ज़्यादा तार-बेतार
उन पर कुछ दूसरी तरह के वार्तालाप
महज़ व्यापार महज़ लेनदेन ख़रीद-फ़रोख़्त की आवाज़ें
लगातार अजनबी होती हुई
जहां भी जाता हूं हताशा में कोई नंबर मिलाता हूं
उस आवाज़ के बारे में पूछता हूं जो कहती थी
दरवाज़े खुले हुए हैं तुम यहां रह सकते हो
चले आओ थोड़ी देर के लिए यों ही कभी भी इस अंतरिक्ष में.

This Number Does Not Exist

This number does not exist.
Wherever I go whichever number I dial
At the other end a strange voice says
This number does not exist *yeh number maujood nahin hai*
Not too long ago at this number I used to reach people
Who said: of course we recognize you
There is space for you in this universe

But now this number does not exist it is some old number.
At these old addresses very few people are left
Where at the sound of footsteps doors would be opened
Now one has to ring the bell and wait in apprehension
And finally when one appears
It is possible that he might have changed
Or he might say I am not the one you used to talk to
This is not the number where you would hear out your grief

Wherever I go numbers maps faces seem to be changed
Old diaries are strewn in the gutters
Their names slow-fading in the water
Now other numbers are available more than ever with and
    without wires
But a different kind of conversation on them
Only business only transactions buy-and-sell voices like strangers
Whenever I go I desperately dial a number
And ask for the voice that used to say
The door is open you can stay here
Come along for a while just for the sake of it any time in this
    universe.

translated by Sudeep Sen

गुमशुदा

शहर के पेशाबघरों और अन्य लोकप्रिय जगहों में
उन गुमशुदा लोगों की तलाश के पोस्टर
अब भी चिपके दिखते हैं
जो कई बरस पहले दस या बारह साल की उम्र में
बिना बताये घरों के निकले थे
पोस्टरों के अनुसार उनका क़द मंझोला है
रंग गोरा नहीं गेहुंआ या सांवला है
वे हवाई चप्पल पहने हैं
उनके चेहरे पर किसी चोट का निशान है
और उनकी मांएं उनके बग़ैर रोती रहती हैं
पोस्टरों के अंत में यह आश्वासन भी रहता है
कि लापता की ख़बर देने वाले को मिलेगा
यथासंभव उचित ईनाम

तब भी वे किसी की पहचान में नहीं आते
पोस्टरों में छपी धुंधली तस्वीरों से
उनका हुलिया नहीं मिलता
उनकी शुरुआती उदासी पर
अब तक़लीफ़ें झेलने की ताब है
शहर के मौसम के हिसाब से बदलते गये हैं उनके चेहरे
कम खाते कम सोते कम बोलते
लगातार अपने पते बदलते
सरल और कठिन दिनों को एक जैसा बिताते
अब वे एक दूसरी ही दुनिया में हैं
कुछ कुतूहल के साथ
अपनी गुमशुदगी के पोस्टर देखते हुए
जिन्हें उनके परेशान माता-पिता जब-तब छपवाते रहते हैं
जिनमें अब भी दस या बारह
लिखी होती हैं उनकी उम्र.

The Missing

In the urinals and other frequented places of this city
One still comes across posters of the missing people
Who had left home quietly many years ago
At the age of ten or twelve
They are shown possessing an average height
Complexion wheatish or dark but never fair
They wear rubber slippers
A scar on the face from some old injury
Their mothers still cry for them
Finally it is mentioned that anybody
Providing any news about the missing
Will be suitably rewarded

Yet no one can identify them
They do not resemble the faded images
On those posters anymore
Their initial sadness is now overwritten
With the endurance of suffering
Their faces reflect the changing seasons of the city
They eat little sleep little speak little
Their addresses keep changing
Facing the good and the bad days with equanimity
They are in their own world
Looking with faint curiosity
At the posters recording them as missing
Which their parents still issue from time to time
In which they continue to be
Ten and twelve.

translated by Asad Zaidi

छूट गया है

भारी मन से चले गये हम
तजकर पुरखों का घरबार
पीछे मिट्टी धसक रही है
गिरती पत्थर की बौछार

थोड़ा मुड़कर देखो भाई
कैसे बंद हो रहे द्वार
उनके भीतर छूट गया है
एक-एक कोठार.

Song of the Dislocated

With a heavy heart we left
tore away from the ancestral home

mud slips behind us now
stones fall in a hail

look back a bit brother
how the doors shut themselves

behind each one of them
a room utterly forlorn.

translated by Asad Zaidi

इन सर्दियों में

पिछली सर्दियाँ बहुत कठिन थीं
उन्हें याद करने पर मैं इन सर्दियों में भी सिहरता हूं
हालांकि इस बार दिन उतने कठोर नहीं

पिछली सर्दियों में चली गयी थी मेरी मां
मुझसे एक प्रेमपत्र खो गया था एक नौकरी छूट गयी थी
रातों को पता नहीं कहां-कहां भटकता रहा
कहां-कहां करता रहा टेलीफ़ोन
पिछली सर्दियों में
मेरी ही चीज़ें गिरती रही थीं मुझ पर

इन सर्दियों में पिछली सर्दियों के कपड़े निकालता हूं
कंबल टोपी मोज़े मफ़लर
उन्हें ग़ौर से देखता हूं
सोचता हुआ पिछला समय बीत गया है
ये सर्दियां क्यों होगी मेरे लिए पहले जैसी कठोर.

This Winter

Last winter was difficult
Remembering it I shiver this winter
Though the days are not so severe

Last winter Mother departed
A love letter went missing a job was lost
I don't know where I wandered in the nights
The many telephone calls I made
My own things kept falling
All over me

This season I unpack the clothes worn last year
—Blankets cap socks a muffler—
I gaze at them intently
Sure that those days are past
This winter can't really be as hard.

translated by Asad Zaidi

पुरानी तस्वीरें

पुरानी तस्वीरों में ऐसा क्या है
जो जब दिख जाती हैं तो मैं ग़ौर से देखने लगता हूं
क्या वह सिर्फ़ एक चमकीली युवावस्था है
सिर पर घने बाल नाक-नक़्श कुछ कोमल
जिन पर माता-पिता से पैदा होने का आभास बचा हुआ है
आंखें जैसे दूर तक देखने की उत्सुकता से भरी हुईं
बिना प्रेस किये हुए कपड़े उस दौर के
जब ज़िंदगी ऐसी ही सलवटों में लिपटी हुई थी

इस तस्वीर में मैं हूं अपने वास्तविक रूप में
एक स्वप्न सरीखा चेहरे पर अपना हृदय लिये हुए
अपने ही जैसे बेफ़िक्र दोस्तों के साथ
एक हल्के बादल की मानिंद जो कहीं से तैरता हुआ आया है
और क्षण भर के लिए एक कोने में टिक गया है
कहीं कोई कठोरता नहीं कोई चतुराई नहीं
आंखों में कोई लालच नहीं
यह तस्वीर सुबह एक ढाबे में चाय पीते समय की है
उसके आसपास की दुनिया भी सरल और मासूम है
चाय के कप ढाबे और सुबह की तरह
ऐसी कितनी ही तस्वीरें हैं जिन्हें कभी-कभी
घर आये मेहमानों को दिखलाता हूं

और अब यह क्या है कि मैं अकसर तस्वीरें ख़िचवाने से कतराता हूं
खींचने वाले से कहता हूं रहने दो
मेरा फ़ोटो अच्छा नहीं आता मैं सतर्क हो जाता हूं
जैसे एक आईना सामने रख दिया गया हो
सोचता हूं क्या यह कोई डर है कि मैं पहले जैसा नहीं दिखूंगा
शायद मेरे चेहरे पर झलक उठेंगी इस दुनिया की कठोरताएं
और चतुराइयां और लालच
इन दिनों हर तरफ़ ऐसी ही चीज़ों की तस्वीरें ज़्यादा दिखाई देती हैं
और जिनसे लड़ने की कोशिश में
मैं कभी-कभी इन पुरानी तस्वीरों को ही
हथियार की तरह उठाने की सोचता हूं.

Old Photographs

What is it in these old photographs
When I chance upon them I can't stop looking
Is it the luminosity of youth alone
A full crop of hair a soft-featured face
That still retains the traces of parental gifts
Eyes brimming with eagerness to see deep and far
Un-ironed clothes from those times
When life itself was in wrinkles

In this picture I represent my real self
Dreamlike, wearing my heart on my face
With friends who share the same casualness
A light cloud that comes floating from somewhere
And rests awhile
No hardness no cleverness
No greed in the eyes
The picture is of a morning at a street-corner teashop
The world around it also transparent and simple
Like the teacup, the street, the morning
There are several such pictures that I occasionally show
To people who come visiting

What is this I now avoid being photographed
I say leave it
I don't photograph well
I get uneasy as if
There is a mirror before me
Is it fear that I won't look as I did
Will my face reveal the harshness of the world
The cleverness and greed one sees everywhere these days
To resist this I sometimes try
To use old photographs as only armor.

translated by Asad Zaidi

प्रतिकार

जो कुछ भी था जहां-तहां हर तरफ़
शोर की तरह खिला हुआ
उसे ही लिखता मैं
संगीत की तरह.

My Way

Whatever was registered like noise
here there everywhere
I tried to inscribe
like music

translated by Asad Zaidi

टॉर्च

मेरे बचपन के दिनों में
एक बार मेरे पिता एक सुंदर-सी टॉर्च लाये
जिसके शीशे में गोल खांचे बने हुए थे
जैसे आजकल कारों की हेडलाइट में होते हैं
हमारे इलाक़े में रोशनी की वह पहली मशीन
जिसकी शहतीर एक चमत्कार की तरह रात को दो हिस्सों में बांट देती थी

एक सुबह मेरी पड़ोस की एक दादी ने पिता से कहा
बेटा इस मशीन से चूल्हा जलाने के लिए थोड़ी-सी आग दे दो
पिता ने हंस कर कहा चाची इसमें आग नहीं होती सिर्फ़ उजाला होता है
इसे रात होने पर जलाते हैं
और इससे पहाड़ के ऊबड़-खाबड़ रास्ते साफ़ दिखाई देते हैं
दादी ने कहा उजाले में थोड़ा आग भी रहती तो कितना अच्छा था
मुझे रात से ही सुबह चूल्हा जलाने की फिक्र रहती है
पिता को कोई जवाब नहीं सूझा वे ख़ामोश रहे देर तक

इतने वर्ष बाद वह घटना टॉर्च की वह रोशनी
आग मांगती दादी और पिता की ख़ामोशी चली आती है
हमारे व़क़्त की विडंबना में कविता की तरह.

Torchlight

Back when I was a child
my father once brought home a torch
the patterns on its glass somewhat like headlights of today's cars
It was the first machine of light in our parts
as its beam fell, like a miracle night parted into two.

One morning a granny from the neighborhood appeared at the
    door
—Son, give me a little fire from this machine to light my stove.
Father smiled—Auntie, this has no fire, just the light
We switch it on only in the dark night to make
the rugged mountain paths visible.
Oh—the grandma said—how good it would be if there were some
    fire too
as night falls I worry for making the fire in the morning.
Father fell silent for a long moment.

After all these years that light from the torch
the granny's demand of fire and Father's helplessness keep
    returning
like a poem in the irony of our time.

translated by Asad Zaidi

सपना

मैं गिरा एकाएक
जैसे सपने से
जैसे चलते-चलते कोई गिरता है
सड़क पर अधबीच

यह मेरी त्वचा के गिरने का सपना था
अपनी आत्मा सहित
मुंह और रोंओं के गिरने का सपना
मेरी गृहस्थी गिरी मेरे साथ
जेब में रखी हुई चीज़ें
जिन्हें मैं बार-बार निकालकर
रखता था फिर जेब में

गिरते गये अब तक कमाये
तमाम मेरे अनुभव
रोने-धोने की आवाज़ें गिरीं साथ-साथ
किसी ने गिरा दिये मेरे कपड़े भी
बारिश और हवा से दूर
गिरता रहा मैं धरती
और रसातल से दूर

गिरते हुए उसकी एक झलक
देखी मैंने
जो हंसते हुए मुझे गिरा रहा था
लगातार.

A Dream

I fell all of a sudden
as if out of a dream
as one trips and falls
on the street

It was a dream of my skin falling away
along with my soul
A dream of mouth and hair falling
my home fell along with me
Things I stuffed in my pocket
took out and
put back again

Moments fell relentless
all that I had been through
Down fell sounds of sobbing and weeping
Someone flung down
My clothing as well
Beyond wind and rain
I tumbled past earth
and the realm beneath

Still falling I saw
a flash
the one pushing me down laughing
and laughing.

translated by Christi Merrill

अभिनय

एक गहन आत्मविश्वास से भरकर
सुबह निकल पड़ता हूं घर से
ताकि सारा दिन आश्वस्त रह सकूं
एक आदमी से मिलते हुए मुस्कराता हूं
वह एकाएक देख लेता है मेरी उदासी
एक से तपाक-से हाथ मिलाता हूं
वह जान जाता है मैं भीतर से हूं अशांत
एक दोस्त के सामने ख़ामोश बैठ जाता हूं
वह कहता है तुम दुबले बीमार क्यों दिखते हो
जिन्होंने मुझे कभी घर में नहीं देखा
वे कहते हैं अरे आप टीवी पर दिखे थे एक दिन

बाज़ारों में घूमता हूं निश्शब्द
डिब्बों में बंद हो रहा है पूरा देश
पूरा जीवन बिक्री के लिए
एक नयी रंगीन किताब है जो मेरी कविता के
विरोध में आयी है
जिसमें छपे सुंदर चेहरों को कोई कष्ट नहीं
जगह-जगह नृत्य की मुद्राएं हैं विचार के बदले
जनाब एक पूरी फ़िल्म है लंबी
आप ख़रीद लें और भरपूर आनंद उठायें

शेष जो कुछ है अभिनय है
चारों ओर आवाज़ें आ रही हैं
मेकअप बदलने का भी समय नहीं है
हत्यारा एक मासूम के कपड़े पहनकर चला आया है
वह जिसे अपने पर गर्व था
एक ख़ुशामदी की आवाज़ में गिड़गिड़ा रहा है
ट्रेजडी है संक्षिप्त लंबा प्रहसन
हरेक चाहता है किस तरह झपट लूं
सर्वश्रेष्ठ अभिनेता का पुरस्कार.

An Act

I shore up confidence each morning
as I set out from home
hoping to maintain my composure
I meet a man and smile
he suddenly sees my sorrow
Eagerly I shake hands with another
who senses the agony deep inside me
I sit with a friend in silence
He says you look sickly and gaunt
Those who never set foot in my house
say oh we saw you on TV the other day

I wander mute through bazaars
A whole country's being packed into boxes
Life itself for sale
A slick new book has appeared in the stands
slighting my poetry
Those glossy faces look untroubled
Dancers strike poses thoughtlessly
Yessir it's all a big movie
Buy it now
Satisfaction guaranteed

The rest is nothing but an act
Voices sound from every direction
No time to change the makeup even
The murderer enters wearing the guise of innocence
The wicked preach a message of love
He who was so dignified
now blubbers and pleads
Tragedy seldom appears the farce plays long
All of them trying to grab
the Award for Best Actor.

translated by Christi Merrill

चेहरा

मां मुझे पहचान नहीं पायी
जब मैं घर लौटा
सर से पैर तक धूल से सना हुआ

मां ने धूल पोंछी
उसके नीचे कीचड़
जो सूखकर सख़्त हो गया था साफ़ किया
फिर उतारे लबादे और मुखौटे
जो मैं पहने हुए था पता नहीं कब से
उसने एक और परत निकालकर फेंकी
जो मेरे चेहरे से मिलती थी

तब दिखा उसे मेरा चेहरा
वह सन्न रह गयी
वहां सिर्फ़ एक ख़ालीपन था
या एक घाव
आड़ी-तिरछी रेखाओं से ढंका हुआ.

My Face

Mother didn't recognize me
when I came back home
covered in dirt from head to toe

Mother wiped away the dirt
and the dried-out mud beneath
She scrubbed awhile longer
Then peeled away the robes and masks
I'd put on
who knows how long ago
She stripped away another layer
one just like my face

As it appeared before her
she drew back stunned
Seeing nothing there but emptiness
a gaping wound
cross-hatched with lines.

translated by Christi Merrill

सभ्यता

हम जानते हैं कि एक आदमी अब भी किसी अदृश्य खोह में अपने तीर-कमान के साथ लड़ाई का अभ्यास कर रहा है. जब कभी भूल से वह नंग-धड़ंग दिख जाता है तो हमारे तैयार कैमरे उसके फ़ोटो ले लेते हैं. कहते हैं हमारे घरों में पहले यही आदमी अपने विशाल कुनबे के साथ रहता था. वे मुखौटों की पूजा करते थे और समुद्र और चिड़ियों से बात करना उनका प्रमुख काम था. हमने उनके मुखौटों की जगह अपने मुखौटे रखे और उनके तीर-कमानों को मौजूदा समय के लिए बेकार मानकर अपने पास जमा कर लिया. उनकी चिड़ियां हमारे पैरों पर गिर पड़ीं.

वे लोग कहां चले गये इस बारे में विद्वानों के अलग-अलग मत हैं. शायद वे समुद्र में डूबे या चिड़ियों की मौत ने या हमारे मुखौटों ने ही उन्हें मार डाला. बहरहाल कुछ का कहना है कि इस सिलसिले में एक भीषण युद्ध हुआ और जब उस कुनबे का एक ही आदमी बचा रह गया तो हमने मुखौटा और तीर-कमान लौटा दिये और उसे दूर किसी गुफा में भेज दिया. सभ्यता यही कहती थी कि एक आदमी ज़रूर बचा रहे तस्वीरों में नहीं बल्कि नंगा जीता-जागता कभी-कभी दिखता हुआ.

Civilization

We believe a man must be out there still, in some unknown cave readying his bow for battle. If he should be sighted our cameras rush to record his nakedness. It is said that he lived in our houses once with his entire clan. They worshiped masks and worried about nothing but talking to the birds and the sea. We put our masks on them in place of theirs and took their bows, useless in this modern day and age, for our own purposes. One by one their birds fell at our feet.

Scholars have many theories about where they have gone. Perhaps they were drowned at sea or disappeared with the birds or maybe our masks were too much for them. However some people say a long battle was fought and when only a single clansman survived we gave him back his mask and bow and banished him to a distant cave. Civilization demanded that there be one man there—not just a picture but a living breathing naked thing.

translated by Christi Merrill

तस्वीर

बहुत पहले सिर्फ़ आसमान था जो कई रंगों में बदलता रहता था. उसके नीचे बादल दौड़ते थे. फिर घास उगी और किसी चिड़िया के बोलने की आवाज़ आयी. कहीं से धीमी बांसुरी सुनाई दी. रात में पहली बार तारे प्रकट हुए और बहुत पास आ गये ताकि हम उन्हें छू सकें. कभी-कभी वे हमसे खेलते और हमारी आंखों में प्रवेश करके चमकने लगते. उस समय पेड़ों के नाम नहीं थे और पत्थर अभी-अभी जन्मे बच्चों की तरह सोये रहते थे. रात को कुछ रोशनियां जलतीं जिनके बारे में विश्वास था कि वे आनेवाले संकटों को भगा देती हैं.

अब यह सब हमारी स्मृति में है. छाते की तरह तना आसमान दूर टंके तारे अपनी जगह स्थिर पेड़ और चिड़ियां जो उड़ती नहीं हैं और पत्थर जिनका बचपन ख़त्म हो चुका है. एक फ़्रेम में जड़ी यह हमारी प्रिय तस्वीर है. रात में चमकती रोशनियों के बारे में हम कहते हैं वे हमारे गांव की आंखें हैं.

A Picture

Long ago there was only sky of ever-changing colors with clouds racing underneath. Then grass sprouted and a bird began to sing. The sound of a flute floated in the air. In the night for the first time the stars appeared so close that we could touch them. Sometimes they joined us in play and twinkled in our eyes. Trees had no names then and the stones used to sleep like newborn children. The lights that burn at night were thought to chase away whatever threatened.

Now all this has been stored in our memory: the sky opens out like an umbrella the stars are stuck in their faraway places the trees and the flying birds are no more and the innocence of stones has come to an end. This is our precious picture we've put in a frame. Looking at the night's twinkling lights we call them the eyes of our village.

translated by Christi Merrill

मांगना

जब भी ख़ुद पर निगाह डालता हूं
पलक झपकते ही मां स्मृति में लौट आती है
मैं याद करता हूं कि उसने मुझे जन्म दिया था
कभी-कभी लगता है वह मुझे लगातार जनमती रही
पिता ने मुझ पर पैसे लुटाये और कहा
शहरों में भटकते हुए कहीं तुम घर की सुध लेना भूल न जाओ
दादा ने पिता को नसीहत दी
जैसा हुनरमंद मैंने तुम्हें बनाया उसी तरह अपने बेटे को बनाओ

दोस्तों ने मेरी पीठ थपथपायी
मुझे उधार दिया और कहा उधार प्रेम की कैंची नहीं हुआ करती
जिससे मैंने प्रेम किया
उसने कहा मेरी छाया में तुम जितनी देर रह पाओ
उतना ही तुम मनुष्य बन सकोगे
किताबों ने कहा हमें पढ़ो
ताकि तुम्हारे भीतर चीज़ों को बदलने की बेचैनी पैदा हो सके

अजीबोग़रीब है जीवन का हाल
वह अब भी भटकता है और जगह-जगह दस्तक देता है
मांगता रहता है अपने लिए
कभी जन्म कभी प्रेम कभी हुनर कभी उधार
कभी बेचैनी कभी प्रेम.

Asking for Favors

When I glance at my reflection
in a blink I recall my mother
remember her giving birth to me
as if she were always bringing me into being
Father lavished money on me and said
Don't forget those at home while you wander in the cities
Grandfather advised my father
Give your son all the abilities I have given you

Friends patted me on the back
Lent me money insisting this loan won't be scissors to our bond
the one I loved
said the longer you stay in my shadow
the more human you'll become
the books said read us
and a restiveness will rise up inside you for change

It's stranger than strange this life
It wanders and knocks at random doors
asking for favors
sometimes for money for abilities for loans for birth itself
sometimes for restiveness sometimes for love.

translated by Christi Merrill

शहर फिर से

इतने समय से तुम क्या खोजते हो इस शहर में
जहां एक धुंधली युवावस्था में
तुम पत्थर की तरह लुढ़कते हुए आये थे
तुम्हें मिली एक ख़ाली जगह एक रात और रात के लिए बिस्तर
यहीं तुम्हें दिखी अपनी स्पष्ट ग़रीबी यहीं मिला अपना अहंकार
यह कौन-सी सभ्यता थी कौन-सा समय
वे किसकी रोशनियां थीं जो तुम्हारे आगे-पीछे चमकती रहती थीं
तुम शहर के भीतर प्रवेश करना चाहते थे उसके रक्त में
उसकी रातों में जिसकी सड़कें कई-कई हाथों से तुम्हें छूती थीं

और अब सुबह उठकर तुम देखते हो
जैसे यह कोई दूसरी जगह दूसरा शहर हो
तुम्हारी सड़कें धुंधली-सी हवा में झूलती हुईं दिखती हैं
तुम्हारे चौराहे अदृश्य हो चुके
वे घर ज़मींदोज़ हो गये जहां तुम चले आते थे
वे लोग भी उन पतों पर नहीं रहते जो तुम्हारी डायरी में दर्ज हैं

अब जहां तुम एक शाश्वत आपाधापी में चलते हो
चमकती हुई चीज़ों के बीच से
हांफते सीढ़ियां चढ़ते-उतरते कभी-कभी हंसते दिखते हो
किताबें और दवाएं ख़रीदते हुए
पैसे खोजने के लिए बार-बार अपनी जेबें टटोलते
जैसे देर हो गयी हो और समय निकला जा रहा हो
वह कोई और ही शहर है जहां तुम होना नहीं चाहते
फिर भी तुम्हें होना होता है तकलीफ़देह सड़कों चौराहों के बीच
तमाम चीज़ों के पिछवाड़े
आज और अभी इस तरह जैसे यह कोई पुरानी बात हो

और जब तुम एक दिन झोला-बिस्तर उठाकर यहां से छूटने के लिए
निकलते हो तो पाते हो तुम्हारे और शहर के बीच कोई नहीं है
लोग जा चुके हैं सड़कें चौराहे सब कुछ एक स्थिर बिंब में ठहरा हुआ है
हवा का एक झोंका आता है आसमान का एक हिस्सा
तुम्हारे चेहरे का स्पर्श करता है दूर एक तारा चमकता है
और इतने पास आ जाता है जैसे वह इस शहर का प्रकाश हो

The City, Again

What have you been searching for all this time in this city
where you arrived in the haze of your youth
tumbling over yourself like a stone
You found a vacant place and a mattress for the night
It was here you saw your poverty clearly and found your self
Which civilization was it which time
whose lights shone all around you
You wanted inside the city to enter its very lifeblood
wanted into its nights whose streets
touched you with so many hands

Now you wake in the morning and look
as if this were some other place another city
Your streets shimmer in the haze
your avenues have disappeared
homes you used to visit have been razed
people in your diary no longer live at those addresses

Now you run in an eternal hurry
in between all the sparkly things
climbing up and down stairs panting sometimes smiling
buying books and medicine
groping in your pockets searching for change
as if you were late and running out of time
It is now another city one where you no longer want to be
And still have to be here on these mean streets and avenues
always in the back
as if right now this very moment were a thing of the past

And when you pack your bags all set to rid yourself of the place
you find that there is no one between you and the city
People have left the streets the avenues everything held in a still
    image
A gust of wind tosses down a piece of sky
touches your face a star shines in the distance

और तुम्हारा कोई पुराना स्वप्न इस तरह जीवित हो उठता है
कि तुम उसे छू सकते हो
तब तुम सड़क के किनारे एक पत्थर पर बैठ जाते हो
और सोचते हो उस शहर में अब भी पहुंचा जा सकता है
जिसकी खोज में तुम यहां आये थे
एक पत्थर की तरह कहीं से लुढ़कते हुए.

and comes so near it seems one of the city lights
Just like that one of your old dreams comes to life
as if you could touch it
then you sit down on one of the stones along the road
and think you can still reach that city
the one you came looking for
tumbling along like a stone.

translated by Christi Merrill

नये युग में शत्रु

अंततः हमारा शत्रु भी एक नये युग में प्रवेश करता है
अपने जूतों कपड़ों और मोबाइलों के साथ
वह एक सदी का दरवाज़ा खटखटाता है
और उसके तहख़ाने में चला जाता है
जो इस सदी और सहस्राब्दी की ही तरह अथाह और अज्ञात है
वह जीत कर आया है और जानता है कि उसकी लड़ाइयां बची हुई हैं
हमारा शत्रु किसी एक जगह नहीं रहता
लेकिन हम जहां भी जाते हैं पता चलता है वह और कहीं रह रहा है
अपनी पहचान को उसने हर जगह अधिक घुला-मिला दिया है
जो लोग ऊंची जगहों में भव्य कुर्सियों पर बैठे हुए दिखते हैं
वे शत्रु नहीं सिर्फ़ उसके कारिंदे हैं
जिन्हें वह भर्ती करता रहता है
ताकि हम उसे खोजने की कोशिश न करें

वह अपने को कंप्यूटरों टेलीविज़नों मोबाइलों
आइपैडों की जटिल आंतों के भीतर फैला देता है
किसी महंगी गाड़ी के भीतर उसकी छाया नज़र आती है
लेकिन वहां पहुंचने पर दिखता है वह वहां नहीं है
बल्कि किसी दूसरी और ज़्यादा नयी गाड़ी में बैठ कर चल दिया है
कभी लगता है वह किसी फ़ैशन परेड में शिरकत कर रहा है
लेकिन वहां सिर्फ़ बनियानों और जांघियों का ढेर दिखाई देता है
हम सोचते हैं शायद वह किसी ग़रीब के घर पर हमला करने चला गया है
लेकिन वह वहां से भी जा चुका है
वहां एक परिवार अपनी ग़रीबी में से झांकता हुआ टेलीविजन देख रहा
जिस पर एक रंगीन कार्यक्रम आ रहा है

हमारे शत्रु के पास बहुत से फ़ोन नंबर हैं ढेरों मोबाइल
वह लोगों को सूचना देता है आप जीत गये हैं
एक विशाल प्रतियोगिता में आपका नाम निकल आया है
आप बहुत सारा कर्ज़ ले सकते हैं बहुत-सा सामान ख़रीद सकते हैं
एक अकल्पनीय उपहार आपका इंतज़ार कर रहा है
लेकिन पलट कर फ़ोन करने पर कुछ नहीं सुनाई देता

Enemy in the New Era

Finally our enemy too has entered this new era
with his shoes clothes and mobiles
He knocks on the door of the century
and hides in its basement
as unfathomable and unknown as this century this millennium
He came conquering and still has more fight in him
Our enemy doesn't live in one place
wherever we go realize he is somewhere else
as soon as we see him he has melded with the place
the high-placed people who sit in proper chairs
they are not the enemy simply his associates
He keeps them in his pay
so we won't try to find him

He seeps into all the intricate entrails of the computers
the televisions the mobiles the iPads
We glimpse his shadow in an expensive car
But as soon as we come near he is gone
has sped off in an even newer pricier car
Sometimes it looks like he's on the fashion circuit
but one that only models heaps of undershirts underpants and
    makeup
We may think he has descended upon the home of a poor family
But he has already come and gone
Left a family in their poverty staring at a television
showing a colorful program.

Our enemy has lots of phone numbers piles of mobiles
He informs people you have won
Your name was selected in a big contest
You can ask for a huge loan buy countless things
An unbelievable complimentary gift awaits you
But when you return the call there is no voice at the other end

हमारा शत्रु कभी हमसे नहीं मिलता सामने नहीं आता
हमें ललकारता नहीं
हालांकि उसके आने-जाने की आहट हमेशा बनी रहती है
कभी-कभी उसका संदेश आता है कि अब कहीं शत्रु नहीं है
हम सब एक दूसरे के मित्र हैं
आपसी मतभेद भुलाकर आइए हम एक ही प्याले से पियें
वसुधैव कुटुंबकम्हमारा विश्वास है
धन्यवाद और शुभरात्रि.

Our enemy never meets us won't face us squarely
Doesn't shout in our face
Nevertheless we hear him come and go
Sometimes he announces that there is no longer an enemy
We are all friends
Let us forget our differences and drink from the same glass
We believe in the Vasudhaiva Kutumbakam
Thank you and good night.

translated by Christi Merrill

नया बैंक

नया बैंक पुराने बैंक की तरह नहीं है
उसमें पुराने बैंक की कोई छाया नहीं है
उसका लोहे की सलाख़ों वाला दरवाज़ा और उसका अंधेरा नहीं है
लॉकर और स्ट्रांगरूम नहीं है
जिसकी चाभियां वह ख़ुद से भी छिपाकर रखता था
वह एक सपाट और रोशन जगह है विशाल कांच की दीवार के पार
एअरकंडीशनर भी बहुत तेज़ है
जहां लोग हांफते पसीना पोंछते आते हैं
और तुरंत कुछ राहत महसूस करते हैं

नये बैंक में एक ठंढी पारदर्शिता है
नया बैंक अपने को हमेशा चमका कर रखता है
उसका फ़र्श लगातार साफ़ किया जाता है
वह अपने आसपास ठेलों पर सस्ती चीज़ें बेचने वालों को भगा देता है
और वहां कारों के लिए कर्ज़ देने वाली गुमटियां खोल देता है
बैंक के भीतर मेजें-कुर्सियां और लोग इस तरह टिके हैं
जैसे वे अभी-अभी आये हों उनकी कोई जड़ें न हों यह सब अस्थायी हो
नया बैंक पुराने बैंक से कोई भाईचारा महसूस नहीं करता
वह उसे कहीं दूर ढकेल देना चाहता है

नये बैंक में वे ख़ज़ांची नहीं हैं जो महान गणितज्ञों की तरह बैठे होते थे
किसी अंधेरे से रहस्यमय पूंजी को निकाल लाते थे
और एक प्रमेय की तरह हल कर देते थे
वे प्रबंधक नहीं हैं
जो बूढ़े लोगों की पेंशन का हिसाब संभाल कर रखते थे
नया बैंक सिर्फ़ दिये जानेवाले कर्ज़
और लिये जानेवाले ब्याज का हिसाब रखता है
प्रोसेसिंग शुल्क मासिक क़िस्त पेमेंट चार्जेज़ चक्रवृद्धि ब्याज
लेट पेमेंट चार्जेज और पैनल्टी वसूलता है
और एक जासूस की तरह देखता रहता है कि कौन अमीर हो रहा है
किसका पैसा कम हो रहा है कौन दिवालियेपन के कगार पर है
और किसका खाता बंद करने का समय आ गया है.

The New Bank

The new bank is not like the old one
No shade like the old bank
Not the iron-grilled doors or the old darkness
No *lockers* or *strongroom*
whose keys the bank keeps hidden
The new bank is a smooth gleaming place beyond a vast glass wall
The air conditioner is so strong
people arrive panting and wiping away sweat
and immediately find relief

In the new bank there is a veneer of coldness
The new bank always keeps itself sparkly
its floor is continuously cleaned
It chases off the carts nearby selling cheap little things
and replaces them with stalls for car loans
Tables chairs people are installed inside the bank as if
they just arrived have no roots are completely unmoored
The new bank feels no solidarity with the old bank
would rather drive it off someplace far away

There are no cashiers in the new bank presiding like
    mathematicians
extracting mysterious funds from the darkness
and offering solutions the way one would advance a theorem
These aren't the managers
who watch over the pensions of the elderly
The new bank only releases loans
and keeps account of interest due
monthly installments *processing* fees compound interest
late payment charges and penalties
and keeps watch like a detective ferreting out who has grown rich
whose money is running low who is on the brink of bankruptcy
and whose ledger is about to be closed.

translated by Christi Merrill

गुजरात के मृतक का बयान

पहले भी शायद मैं थोड़ा-थोड़ा मरता था
बचपन से ही धीरे-धीरे जीता और मरता था
जीवित रहने की अंतहीन खोज ही था जीवन
जब मुझे जलाकर पूरा मार दिया गया
तब तक मुझे आग के ऐसे इस्तेमाल के बारे में पता नहीं था
मैं रंगता था कपड़े तानेबाने रेशे
टूटी-फूटी चीज़ों की मरम्मत करता था
गढ़ता था लकड़ी के हिंडोले और गरबा के रंगीन डांडिये
अल्युमिनियम के तारों से बच्चों के लिए छोटी-छोटी साइकिलें बनाता
इसके बदले में मुझे मिल जाती थी एक जोड़ी चप्पल एक तहमद
अपनी ग़रीबी में दिन भर उसे पहनता रात को ओढ़ लेता
आधा अपनी औरत को देता हुआ

मेरी औरत मुझसे पहले ही जला दी गयी
वह मुझे बचाने के लिए मेरे आगे खड़ी हो गयी थी
और मेरे बच्चों को मारा जाना तो पता ही नहीं चला
वे इतने छोटे थे उनकी कोई चीख़ भी सुनाई नहीं दी
मेरे हाथों में जो हुनर था पता नहीं उसका क्या हुआ
मेरे हाथों का ही पता नहीं क्या हुआ
वे अब सिर्फ़ जले हुए ढांचे हैं एक जली हुई देह पर चिपके हुए
उनमें जो हरकत थी वही थी उनकी कला
और मुझे इस तरह मारा गया
जैसे एक साथ बहुत से दूसरे लोग मारे जा रहे हों
मेरे जीवित होने का कोई बड़ा मक़सद नहीं था
लेकिन मुझे इस तरह मारा गया
जैसे मुझे मारना कोई बड़ा मक़सद हो

और जब मुझसे पूछा गया तुम कौन हो
क्या छिपाये हो अपने भीतर एक दुश्मन का नाम
कोई मज़हब कोई तावीज़
मैं कुछ कह नहीं पाया मेरे भीतर कुछ नहीं था
सिर्फ़ एक रंगरेज़ एक मिस्त्री एक कारीगर एक कलाकार
जब मैं अपने भीतर मरम्मत कर रहा था किसी टूटी हुई चीज़ की
जब मेरे भीतर दौड़ रहे थे
अल्युमिनियम के तारों की साइकिल के नन्हे पहिये

One of Gujarat's Dead Speaks

Earlier too I died a little
from childhood I slowly lived and slowly died
The endless search of my life was life itself
When they burned me to death
I hadn't even known fire could be used this way
I used to dye cloth and fiber
repaired broken wares
carved wooden swings and colorful sticks for the garba dance
fashioned little bicycles from aluminum wire
In return I was given a pair of sandals a cloth for my waist
covered my poverty with it by day and curled up in it by night
sharing half with my woman

My woman was set on fire first
She had stood in front to save me
and never knew how our children died
They were so small their cries couldn't even be heard
No one knows what happened to the talent in my hands
or what happened to my hands
Now they are just bones in a burnt body
their art was in how they moved
Though I was killed as if
a great number were being killed alongside me
there was no larger purpose to my living
But I was killed
as if there were great purpose to the killing

And when I was asked who are you
what are you hiding inside the name of what enemy
which faith which amulet
I was unable to say there was nothing inside me
only a dyer a carpenter a craftsman an artist
When I was repairing some little thing inside me
when something was running inside me
on the tiniest little tires of an aluminum wire bicycle

तभी मुझ पर गिरी एक आग बरसे पत्थर
और जब मैंने आख़िरी इबादत में अपने हाथ फैलाये
तब तक मुझे पता नहीं था बंदगी का कोई जवाब नहीं आता

अब जब कि मैं मारा जा चुका हूं मिल चुका हूं
मृतकों की उस मनुष्यता में
जो जीवित मनुष्यों से भी ज़्यादा सच्ची ज़्यादा स्पंदित है
तुम्हारी जीवित बर्बर दुनिया में न लौटने के लिए
मुझे और मत मारो और मत जलाओ न कहने के लिए
अब जबकि मैं महज़ एक मनुष्याकार हूं एक मिटा हुआ चेहरा
एक मरा हुआ नाम
तुम जो कुछ हैरत और कुछ ख़ौफ़ से मेरी ओर देखते हो
क्या पहचानने की कोशिश करते हो
क्या तुम मुझमें अपने किसी स्वजन को खोजते हो
किसी मित्र-परिचित को या ख़ुद अपने को
अपने चेहरे में लौटते देखते हो किसी चेहरे को.

just then a scatter of fire rained over me
and when I reached out in final prayer
I did not know that prayers are never answered

Now that I have been murdered have witnessed
such humanity in the dead
more truthful and more vibrant
than the humanity of the living
never to return to the barbaric world of the living
never to say again don't burn me don't kill me
Now that I am merely the image of a human
a face smudged out a name that has died
You who stare at me with shock and fear
what are you trying to see in my face
Do you search for someone close to you in me
The face of a friend a familiar maybe your own
Do you see my face in your face?

translated by Christi Merrill

यथार्थ इन दिनों

मैं जब भी यथार्थ का पीछा करता हूं
देखता हूं वह भी मेरा पीछा कर रहा है मुझसे तेज़ भाग रहा है
घर हो या बाज़ार हर जगह उसके दांत चमकते हुए दिखते हैं
अंधेरे में रोशनी में
घबराया हुआ मैं नींद में जाता हूं तो वह वहां मौजूद होता है
एक स्वप्न से निकलकर बाहर आता हूं
तो वह वहां भी पहले से घात लगाये हुए रहता है

यथार्थ इन दिनों इतना चौंधियाता हुआ है
कि उससे आंखें मिलाना मुश्किल है
मैं उसे पकड़ने के लिए आगे बढ़ता हूं
तो वह हिंस्र जानवर की तरह हमला करके निकल जाता है
सिर्फ़ कहीं-कहीं उसके निशान दिखाई देते हैं
किसी सड़क पर जंगल में पेड़ के नीचे
एक झोपड़ी के भीतर एक उजड़ा हुआ चूल्हा एक ढही हुई छत
छोड़कर चले गये लोगों का एक सुनसान

एक मरा हुआ मनुष्य इस समय
जीवित मनुष्य की तुलना में कहीं ज़्यादा कह रहा है
उसके शरीर से बहता हुआ रक्त
शरीर के भीतर दौड़ते हुए रक्त से कहीं ज़्यादा आवाज़ कर रहा है
एक तेज़ हवा चल रही है
और विचारों स्वप्नों स्मृतियों को
फटे हुए काग़ज़ों की तरह उड़ा रही है
एक अंधेरी-सी काली सी चीज़
हिंस्र पशुओं से भरी हुई एक रात चारों ओर इकट्ठा हो रही है
एक लुटेरा एक हत्यारा एक दलाल
आसमानों पहाड़ों मैदानों को लांघता हुआ आ रहा है
उसके हाथ धरती के मर्म को दबोचने के लिए बढ़ रहे हैं

एक आदिवासी को उसके जंगल से खदेड़ने का ख़ाका बन चुका है
विस्थापितों की एक भीड़
अपनी बचीखुची गृहस्थी को पोटलियों में बांध रही है
उसे किसी अज्ञात भविष्य की ओर ढकेलने की योजना तैयार है
ऊपर आसमान में एक विकराल हवाई जहाज़ बम बरसाने के लिए तैयार है

Reality These Days

When I chase after reality
I see it chasing after me running faster than me
at home or in the market I see its glinting teeth everywhere
in the dark in the light
I go to sleep afraid he'll be there
I slip out of a dream
to find him already there waiting for a chance to strike

These days reality is so dazzling
It's difficult to look right at it
I set out to catch it
but it has attacked and run off like a wild animal
only traces of it are seen here and there
on the street underneath a tree in the wild
inside a hut in an abandoned hearth a collapsed roof
a place people have left deserted

A dead man right now
has a lot more to say than anyone living
The blood oozing from his body
makes more noise than the blood in his body
A stiff wind is blowing
and ideas dreams memories
are being chased along like scraps of paper
a darkish blackish thing
a night is gathering filled with dangerous beasts[1]
a swindler a murderer a hustler
leaping over the sky the mountains the fields
its hand reaching out to seize the earth's vitals

A plan has already been made to drive a tribe from its jungle
a crowd of displaced persons
bundles up whatever remains of their household effects
blueprints drawn to push them into an unknown future
Up in the sky a fearsome airplane is ready with a bomb

नीचे घाटी में एक आत्मघाती दस्ता
अपने सुंदर नौजवान शरीरों पर बम और मिसालें बांधे हुए है
दुनिया के राष्ट्राध्यक्ष अंगरक्षक सुरक्षागार्ड सैनिक अर्धसैनिक बल
गोलियों बंदूकों रॉकेटों से लैस हो रहे हैं
यथार्थ इन दिनों बहुत ज्यादा यथार्थ है
उसके शरीर से ज्यादा दिखाई दे रहा है उसका रक्त.

---

1. निराला की एक कविता पंक्ति 'शिशिर की शर्वरी हिंस्र पशुओं से भरी' का संदर्भ

down below in the valley a platoon of suicide bombers
bombs and *missiles* tied onto their beautiful young bodies
world leaders with their bodyguards security guards military
    paramilitary forces
are being equipped with bullets guns *rocket* launchers
Reality is too much of a reality these days
its blood more visible than its body.

---

1. In the context of Nirala's poem: "shishir ki sharvari / hinsra pashuon se
   bhari" (the night of the winter / full of violent beasts)

translated by Christi Merrill

Acknowledgments

I am indebted to my friends and translators, some of whom are well-known poets in their own right. My special thanks to the prestigious poets Arvind Krishna Mehrotra, Vishnu Khare, Girdhar Rathi, Asad Zaidi, Sudeep Sen, Akhil Katyal, Nirupama Dutt, and Sarabjeet Garcha, who have been very generous with the time and attention they gave to my poems. This selection would not have been possible without them.

I am also grateful to Professor Rupert Snell and Professor Robert Hueckstedt, who were "instantly inspired" to translate some of my poems; and a special thank you to the well-known translator Christi Merrill, who has been a friend and translator of my poems since we met at the Iowa International Writing Program in 1991. I am most grateful to the distinguished poet and translator of European poetry, the late Daniel Weissbort, who meticulously examined several of the poems included in this collection during a poetry workshop organized by the Sahitya Akademi in New Delhi.

Many of these poems were first published in the periodicals *World Literature Today, Modern Poetry in Translation, Poetry Review, Indian Horizon, Indian Literature, Hindi,* and *The Little Magazine* and in the anthologies *Periplus, Gestures, Signatures, These My Words, India in Verse, Beyond Borders,* and *An Anthology of Modern Hindi Poetry,* among others. Thanks to all the editors.

Finally, my thanks to poet and friend Nikola Madzirov, who wanted my poems to reach a wider audience, and to Peter Conners, Jenna Fisher, Melissa Hall, and Sandy Knight of BOA Editions for their deep interest in bringing out this book. I would also like to thank Marathi poet and friend Hemant Divate, who first published most of these translations in an Indian edition from his press Poetrywala, and Alma Dabral for helping in the preparation of the manuscript.

About the Author

Mangalesh Dabral was born in 1948 in a village in the Tehri Garhwal district of the Himalayan region. He has spent all his adult life as a literary editor at various newspapers published in Delhi and other north Indian cities. His books include five collections of poems, titled *Pahar Par Laltein* (*Lantern on the Mountain*, 1981), *Ghar Ka Rasta* (*The Way Home*, 1981), *Hum Jo Dekhate Hain* (*That Which We See*, 1995), *Aawaaz Bhi Ek Jagah Hai* (*Voice Too Is a Place*, 2000), and *Naye Yug Mein Shatru* (*Enemy in the New Era*, 2014); two collections of literary essays and sociocultural commentary, titled *Lekhak Ki Roti* (*Writer's Bread*, 1998) and *Kavi Ka Akelapan* (*Solitude of a Poet*, 2008); and a book of conversations, *Upkathan* (*Substatement*, 2014). He has also published a travel account, *Ek Baar Iowa* (*Once, Iowa*, 1996), based on his experiences in Iowa, where he resided for three months as a fellow of the International Writing Program in 1991 and gave poetry readings in various American cities.

His poems have been widely translated and published in all major Indian languages and in Russian, German, Dutch, Spanish, French, Italian, Japanese, Polish, Bulgarian, and Portuguese. They have been included in various periodicals, such as *World Literature Today, Modern Poetry in Translation, Poetry Review,* and *The Little Magazine,* and in the anthologies *Periplus* (ed. Daniel Weissbort and Arvind Krishna Mehrotra), *Survival* (ed. Daniel Weissbort and Girdhar Rathi), *Gestures* (an anthology of poems from SAARC countries), *Signatures* (ed. K. Satchidanandan), *Aria* (by Sudeep Sen), *These My Words* (ed. Eunice De Souza and Melanie Silgardo), and *India in Verse* (ed. Antara Dev Sen). *Aawaaz Bhi Ek Jagah Hai* was translated into Italian by Prof. Mariola Offredi under the title *Anche la Voce e un Luogo.*

He participated in the Poetry International Festival, Rotterdam, the Netherlands, in 2008 and Sabad International Poetry Festival, New Delhi, in 2014. He has also given poetry readings in Bulgaria, the then Czechoslovakia, Nepal, Mauritius, Japan, Russia, and various cities in Germany, including on the eve of the Frankfurt Book Fair in 2006.

He has translated into Hindi the poems of Pablo Neruda, Bertolt Brecht, Ernesto Cardenal, Yannis Ritsos, Tadeusz Różewicz, and Zbigniew Herbert, to name a few. He has also worked as a consultant to the National Book Trust, India, and has received a number of awards, including Shamsher Sammaan (1995), Pahal Sammaan (1998), the Sahitya Akademi Award (2000), Delhi Hindi Academy's Sahityakar Samman (2001), and the Kumar Vikal Smriti Award (2008).

About the Translators

Nirupama Dutt is a well-known Punjabi poet, journalist, and translator. She has translated revolutionary Punjabi poet Lal Singh Dil's poetry and autobiography, and a collection of contemporary Punjabi short stories into English, both published by Penguin India.

Sarabjeet Garcha is a bilingual poet, editor, and translator. He has a book of poems in Hindi and two books in English, the latest being *Lullaby of the Ever-Returning* (Poetrywala). He received a fellowship in literature from the Ministry of Culture, Government of India. He is the cofounder and director of Copper Coin, a multilingual indie publishing company.

Robert Hueckstedt is a professor of Hindi and Sanskrit at the University of Virginia. He has translated Mudra Rakshas's novel *Dandavidhan* and two of Uday Prakash's short story collections, including *Short Shorts Long Shots*, into English. His translations from Hindi have appeared in leading literary journals. In 1998 he was awarded a literary translation prize sponsored by the British Centre for Literary Translation.

Akhil Katyal is a young poet and translator. His first book of poems, *Night Charges Extra*, was published by the Writers Workshop, Kolkata. He has a Ph.D. in English literature from the School of Oriental and African Studies, University of London, and teaches at Shiv Nadar University, Greater Noida, India.

Vishnu Khare is an eminent Hindi poet, critic, and translator. He has published several collections of poetry, including *Khud Apni Aankh Se, Sabki Aawaaz Ke Parde Mein*, and *Paathantar*; a book-length English collection of several Hindi poets; a collection of Hindi poetry in German (with Lothar Lutze); collections of Nottebaum, Czesław Miłosz, Wisława Szymborska, and Miklos Radnoti in Hindi; and Finland's national epic, *Kalewala*, in Hindi. He has also written art and cinema criticism for many leading periodicals.

Arvind Krishna Mehrotra is an eminent poet, translator, and anthologist. He is the author of four books of poetry, including *Nine Enclosures, Middle Earth,* and *The Transfiguring Places;* editor of *The Oxford India Anthology of Twelve Modern Indian Poets, Collected Poems in English* by Arun Kolatkar, and *The Last Bungalow: Writings on Allahabad;* and translator of *The Absent Traveller: Prakrit Love Poetry and Songs of Kabir.* He taught English literature at the University of Allahabad, India.

Christi Merrill has a Ph.D. in comparative literature from the University of Iowa. She is associate professor of South Asian Literature and Postcolonial Theory, Asian Languages and Cultures, and Comparative Literature at the University of Michigan. She has translated the famous Rajasthani author Vijaydan Detha's short stories and Dalit author Kaushalya Baisantri's autobiography into English.

Girdhar Rathi is a well-known Hindi poet, editor, translator, and human rights activist. He has published four volumes of poetry, including *Baahar Bheetar* and *Nimitt;* two books of criticism; one travelogue; and co-edited, with Daniel Weissbort, *Survival: An Experience and an Experiment in Translating Modern Hindi Poetry.* He has also translated and edited Hungarian poetry and plays.

Sudeep Sen is a widely recognized English poet, translator, and anthologist. His critically acclaimed books include *New York Times* and *Postmarked India: New and Selected Poems,* among many others. He has edited several important anthologies, including *The HarperCollins Book of English Poetry by Indians,* and received many awards, fellowships, and residencies. He is the editorial director of Aark Arts and editor of *Atlas.*

Rupert Snell is the director of the Hindi-Urdu Flagship and a professor in the Department of Asian Studies, University of Texas, Austin. Known for his textbooks in the Teach Yourself series, he teaches Hindi language at all levels. His publications include *The Eighty-Four Hymns of Hita Harivamsha* and *The Hindi Classical*

Tradition: A Braj Bhasa Reader. Snell's translation of the autobiography of the Hindi poet Harivansh Rai Bachchan, published in 1998 under the title *In the Afternoon of Time*, has received much acclaim.

Asad Zaidi is an acclaimed Hindi poet, critic, and translator. He has published three volumes of poetry, including *Behnein Aur Anya Kavitayen* and *Saamaan Ki Talaash*. He runs the Three Essays Collective, an independent publishing house focused on a wide range of themes in history, politics, culture, education, and media.

◆

The Lannan Translations Selection Series

Ljuba Merlina Bortolani, *The Siege*
Olga Orozco, *Engravings Torn from Insomnia*
Gérard Martin, *The Hiddenness of the World*
Fadhil Al-Azzawi, *Miracle Maker*
Sándor Csoóri, *Before and After the Fall: New Poems*
Francisca Aguirre, *Ithaca*
Jean-Michel Maulpoix, *A Matter of Blue*
Willow, Wine, Mirror, Moon: Women's Poems from Tang China
Felipe Benítez Reyes, *Probable Lives*
Ko Un, *Flowers of a Moment*
Paulo Henriques Britto, *The Clean Shirt of It*
Moikom Zeqo, *I Don't Believe in Ghosts*
Adonis (Ali Ahmad Sa'id), *Mihyar of Damascus, His Songs*
Maya Bejerano, *The Hymns of Job and Other Poems*
Novica Tadić, *Dark Things*
Praises & Offenses: Three Women Poets of the Dominican Republic
Ece Temelkuran, *Book of the Edge*
Aleš Šteger, *The Book of Things*
Nikola Madzirov, *Remnants of Another Age*
Carsten René Nielsen, *House Inspections*
Jacek Gutorow, *The Folding Star and Other Poems*
Marosa di Giorgio, *Diadem*
Zeeshan Sahil, *Light and Heavy Things*
Sohrab Sepehri, *The Oasis of Now*
Dariusz Sośnicki, *The World Shared: Poems*
Nguyen Phan Que Mai, *The Secret of Hoa Sen*
Aleš Debeljak, *Smugglers*
Erez Bitton, *You Who Cross My Path*
Mangalesh Dabral, *This Number Does Not Exist*

For more on the Lannan Translations Selection Series
visit our website:
www.boaeditions.org

◆

Printed in the USA
CPSIA information can be obtained
at www.ICGtesting.com
JSHW082209140824
68134JS00014B/525

9 781942 683124